Multicultural Education

Management Books

Pete Farrell

Published by Scholastic Publications Ltd,
Marlborough House, Holly Walk,
Leamington Spa, Warwickshire CV32 4LS

© 1990 Scholastic Publications Ltd

Written by Pete Farrell
Edited by Christine Lee
Sub-edited by Catherine Baker
Illustrated by Sarah Hedley
Designed by Sue Limb

Designed using Aldus Pagemaker
Processed by Studio Photoset, Leicester
Artwork by Norfolk House Graphic
Designers, Leicester
Printed and bound by Richard Clay Ltd,
Bungay, Suffolk

British Library Cataloguing in Publication Data
Farrell, Peter
    Multicultural education. - (Management books)
    1. Great Britain. Primary Schools. Multicultural education
    I. Title II. Series
    372.0115

    ISBN 0-590-76207-9

Front and back covers designed by Sue Limb

Contents

Introduction

Introduction

At some time in their lives most British schoolchildren, whether in all-white or multi-ethnic schools, will find themselves living, working and mixing with people from a wide variety of racial and cultural backgrounds.

The girl from a small all-white village in Cornwall may go on to higher education in Birmingham, while the boy from a small town in Leicestershire may find a job in Leicester itself where 25 per cent of the population are of Asian descent. Schools should prepare children for the outside world, and the world of twentieth century Britain is multiracial and multicultural. Within that world there is undoubtedly much ignorance, much prejudice, much intolerance and much racism.

Children should be encouraged to value people as people irrespective of their colour, creed or cultural background. All children should be aware of the multicultural society in which we live, of the different groups that make up that society and the contributions made by those groups.

There is a powerful argument that it is in all-white schools that the greatest effort needs to be made. It is in those schools that the myths of immigration need to be dispelled and the realities of prejudice and racism faced.

Multicultural education has been the focus for bitter educational debate and controversy over the last 20 years. At its most extreme, detractors have talked of political conspiracy, bewailed the intrusion of left wing politics into the classroom, decried the pandering to the needs of immigrants over the rights of native-born Britons and flatly denied that there exists such a phenomenon as racism in British society.

Even among its proponents multicultural education has aroused much dissension and division. There have been accusations of 'tokenism' within the classroom: too much attention paid to superficial things like steel bands and exotic foods. There have been accusations of failing to respond adequately to the needs of ethnic minority pupils or failing to challenge the attitudes and images held by white teachers and children.

The terminology itself has caused much acrimony. Should we declare ourselves to be multiculturalists, interculturalists, non-racists or anti-racists? Finding the appropriate label or slogan often seems to be more important than finding something to offer the classroom teacher.

This book is not aimed at the professional multiculturalist or anti-racist. It is aimed at classroom teachers. It has two main objectives. The first is to examine some of the issues behind the multicultural debate and to offer suggestions as to how these can be raised in schools. The second is to look at ways in which theory could be translated into practice.

Chapter One

The issues

Immigration and settlement

I believe it is essential for all teachers to understand the history of Britain as a multicultural, multiracial nation. Like anybody else, teachers are susceptible to popular myths and beliefs.

It is only within the context of the past that we can properly begin to understand the present. For this reason I will begin this chapter with a section on immigrants in Britain over the last 2000 years. The fears expressed now about immigrants, aliens, strange ways and differences have been voiced every time there have been new arrivals who brought with them something unfamiliar: language, religion, food or clothes. However, while previous migrants and settlers have been predominantly white, the more recent arrivals from Asia and the Caribbean are visibly different, and much of the debate about immigration is centred on this difference.

The DES declared in 1977 that 'Our school is now a multicultural, multiracial one and the curriculum should reflect a sympathetic understanding of the different cultures and the races that now make up our society'. A statement like this really means that there is now in Britain a sizeable minority of population which is clearly and recognisably visible by the colour of its skin. This must be the case since any brief examination of British history reveals that we have always been a multiracial and multicultural nation. It is important that teachers both accept and use this to argue against popular myths that immigration is a post World War Two phenomenon.

When Julius Caesar invaded Britain in 55 BC he found a population composed mainly of Celts, Picts and native Britons. Over 100 years later the Roman historian Tacitus observed about the tribes of Britain: 'The red hair and large limbs of Caledonia pointed quite clearly to a German origin, while the dark complexion of the Silures, their usually curly hair and the fact that Spain lies opposite them are evidence that the Iberians crossed over and occupied these parts'.

For the next 400 years Britain was exposed to innumerable imperial influences. Trade routes were opened up, and soldiers from every corner of the Empire, from Cappodocia, Germany, Spain, Gaul and Africa, spent long periods of time in Britain. They brought with them their different clothes, foods, languages and religions.

In AD 410 the last Roman legion was withdrawn from Britain to defend Rome against the Goths and Vandals.

During the next 400 years there were successive waves of invasion. When King Harold met Duke William of Normandy near Hastings in 1066 his army was made up of Britons, Picts, Saxons, Angles and Danes. This could hardly be described as a monolingual, monocultural or monoracial group struggling to preserve some precious homogeneous identity against a foreign invader.

The Norman victory added yet another colour to this cultural rainbow. For a long period after the conquest the rulers of

England spoke French. Anglo-Saxon, the majority language, was treated with scorn and disdain by the ruling class.

The Normans brought more contact with mainland Europe and even encouraged the settlement of other ethnic groups. Jews became money-lenders to the English kings, and weavers and merchants came to England from Flanders. Later Italians from Lombardy succeeded the Jews as royal bankers.

It was inevitable that these groups with their strange customs were not always welcomed. In 1190 there was a massacre of Jews in York and in 1280 the Jews were expelled from England by Edward I. During the Peasants' Revolt of 1380 over 300 Flemish merchants were killed.

By the sixteenth and seventeenth centuries the English began to look outwards. The voyages of Drake, Hawkins, Raleigh and others marked the beginning of the British Empire and the development of the slave trade in Africa.

The seventeenth century in England saw two significant immigrations. In 1655 Oliver Cromwell allowed the return of the Jews, after an official absence of over 350 years, for two reasons. The first was economic (Jewish enterprise and business flair), and the second was religious; the Bible states that the second coming will not take place until there are 'Jews in every nation on earth'.

The last 20 years of the seventeenth century witnessed immigration on a scale perhaps only paralleled in this century. Over 100,000 Protestant Huguenots fled from France to avoid religious persecution. This was at a time when the population of Britain was only about eight million. The Huguenot people were silk weavers, clock and instrument makers, glass, paper and pottery makers, and they settled initially in East Anglia and London.

The accession of George of Hanover to the British throne in 1701 brought another king who, like the Normans, preferred to speak his own native tongue. With the king came German businessmen, artists and musicians.

The next wave of immigration came from closer to home. There had been an Irish community in London since the early seventeenth century. The Industrial Revolution drew even more Irish people to England in their escape from poverty and unemployment. The Irish helped to build canals, then railways and, of course, the cities. The Irish population in 1841 is estimated to have been 400,000. This was greatly increased by the exodus during the potato famine of 1845-1846. Irish migration to Britain was a product of economic necessity and survival. This pattern has continued right up to the present day.

Following Cromwell's decision to allow the Jews to resettle, their numbers had grown steadily. By 1800 there were an estimated 25,000 in Britain. Modern Jewish immigration began in 1881, the year of Czar Nicholas I's assassination. This event was the catalyst for widescale pogroms throughout Russia and Eastern Europe. Jews fled in their thousands to the USA and Britain. By 1905 over 150,000 had arrived.

Their arrival was met with much opposition and virulent anti-Semitism. The right wing press clamoured for immigration controls and likened Whitechapel to Jerusalem. The Aliens Act 1905 effectively blocked any further mass immigration by Jews.

The rise of Fascism in the 1930s, however, led to many Jews again seeking refuge elsewhere. Between 1933 and 1939 some 60,000 settled in Britain.

The post-war period was characterised throughout Europe by movements of people on a vast scale. Millions of refugees, displaced persons and prisoners of war trickled homewards or sought new lives elsewhere in the world. Between 1945 and 1950 more than 450,000 European refugees settled in Britain. Over 150,000 of these were Poles, many of whom had served in the British army. Even 15,000 German prisoners of war were allowed to settle.

During the late 1940s and 1950s there was a massive programme of reconstruction in Britain. This was hindered by a chronic labour shortage. A solution was attempted in the form of a vigorous recruiting campaign across Europe and the Commonwealth. Commonwealth citizens were encouraged to come to Britain, and ethnic minority groups began to arrive in significant numbers.

Over 150,000 West Indians had arrived by 1961. There were also large groups of people from India, Pakistan and what is

now Bangladesh. These were mainly Hindu, Moslem or Sikh. Most of these arrivals were employed as unskilled labour, even though many were well qualified in other spheres.

The 1950s also saw the arrival of Greek and Turkish Cypriots following civil war in Cyprus. In 1956 over 20,000 Hungarians fled to Britain after the uprising in Budapest. Only 500 of these were without employment within three years of their arrival; proof indeed of Britain's capacity to cope with the job demands of the newcomers.

This economic boom also attracted Chinese from Hong Kong and the New Territories. By 1981 there were over 60,000 Chinese living in Britain. After the initial period of acceptance most immigrants encountered hostility, prejudice and overt racism as soon as they began to aspire beyond unskilled labour. The Imperial Act 1914 had established the right of all Commonwealth citizens to settle in Britain. Now, however, there was public and political pressure for restrictive legislation.

The Conservative government of Harold Macmillan passed the Commonwealth Immigrants Act 1962. This was followed by Labour legislation in 1968 which made entry even more difficult. The Immigration Act 1971 ended virtually all immigration for settlement.

The 1970s, however, saw two major migrations to Britain. In 1973 over 50,000 Asians, expelled by Idi Amin from Uganda, came to Britain. In 1979 small numbers of Vietnamese boat people began to arrive, a trend continued through the 1980s.

Many people genuinely believe that the black presence began with post World War Two immigration. Few of us are aware that:

• The Roman emperor Septimius Severus who spent his last three years in Britain until his death in 258 AD was black.

• In the early sixteenth century a small group of Africans were among the court of James IV of Scotland.

• In 1596 Queen Elizabeth I sent the following open letter to the Lord Mayor of London and the mayors of other towns: 'Her majestie understanding that there are of late divers blackamoores brought into this realme of which kinde of people there are already here to manie.... Those kinds of people should be sent forth of the lande.'

• From the 1650s having a black slave in one's household became extremely fashionable.

• In 1764 the *Gentleman's Magazine* estimated the number of black people in London to be 20,000. The majority of these were household servants. This was at a time when the population of England and Wales was 8,500,000.

The educational response

Clearly the order of priority and level of discussion differs from school to school. What is top priority for an inner-city school in Birmingham might be much lower for a rural school in Cornwall. Some schools genuinely believe they already offer equal opportunity for all pupils in terms of race, gender and disability. However, multicultural education is not easily definable either in terms of philosophy or strategy.

Attitudes, philosophies, educational policy and practice have all undergone many changes over the last 30 years. In the 1960s education for a multicultural society meant teaching Asian children English as a second language. In the 1970s it was considered sufficient for schools to recognise and include the celebration of religious festivals. In the 1980s, however, people began to argue that prejudice and racism should be met head-on in all areas of education.

This chapter aims to outline some of the central issues within the debate. The facts already outlined speak for themselves. Britain has always been a multiracial, multicultural society; what Daniel Defoe described as a 'mongrel race'. It is only in the last 35 years, however, that Britain has become a nation with a large visible minority of black and

Asian people. The debate about multicultural education is centred on this fact. Indeed multicultural education is often viewed only as a response to the arrival of Asian and Afro-Caribbean children in British schools in the last 30 or 40 years.

Why is the debate rarely extended to include other groups who have settled in Britain since the beginning of mass education in the 1970s? The answer clearly lies in educational policy. Immigrant children (Jewish, Irish, German, Polish, Ukranian, Italian or Hungarian) were to be absorbed within the educational system with the minimum of fuss. The needs of these children were viewed in terms of language, and scant attention was paid to their varied backgrounds. Their own language was ignored or seen as a hindrance to the acquisition of English. Provision for the teaching of English to these children was negligible. The feeling was that 'they'll soon pick it up', and indeed, they often did.

Once they had the necessary language skills, these children could be assimilated within the school structure and brought to share the same values, aspirations and opportunities of the majority community.

It was generally agreed that this policy worked, and even now some people argue that 'we never had this trouble with Poles' or 'oh, Ukranians - they fitted in quite easily'. It is not surprising then that the arrival of large numbers of children from India, Pakistan, Bangladesh and the Caribbean would lead to a similar response. These children were diagnosed as having a problem which was preventing them from taking full advantage of the educational opportunities on offer; the problem was identified as the lack of English language skills.

The Asian child was perceived as 'backward' rather than potentially bilingual. Afro-Caribbean children presented a more complicated dilemma. They spoke a language which was clearly a form of English but not a standard form. For both groups the answer lay in compensation and correction.

In the early 1960s the Commonwealth Immigrants Advisory Council recommended that special provision be made for the education of immigrant pupils. In reality this meant the development of a system of teaching English as a second language (E2L). Behind this lay the belief that these children would assimilate into British society in much the same way as previous immigrants were perceived to have done. These children were not seen as potential contributors, enhancers or enrichers of their schools. The second report of the Commonwealth Immigrants Advisory Council 1964 declared:

'A national system of education must aim at producing citizens who can take their place in society properly equipped to exercise rights and perform duties the same as those of other citizens. If their parents were brought up in another culture and tradition, children should be encouraged to respect it, but a national system cannot be expected to perpetuate the different values of immigrant groups'.

Far from being seen as having something to offer, immigrant children were often viewed as a threat. The threat lay in their visibility: previous immigrant children had been almost wholly indistinguishable from British-born white children. This had been the key to successful assimilation. Of course in the beginning these children had been different, but within a short time this 'problem' was solved. It was considered that all children were children and thus should be treated exactly the same. It was therefore inappropriate to notice or emphasise cultural, religious or racial differences. Asian and Caribbean children, however, would not 'disappear'. Their numbers were often extremely high in inner-city schools, and fears were expressed that the character of these schools would be radically changed. For many local authorities the solution was to avoid undue concentration in a particular school through a policy of busing children to outlying schools.

Challenges to this model of assimilation began to grow during the late 1960s and early 1970s. It was argued that the reality of assimilation meant that whites stayed the same while black and Asian people were forced to discard their identity. Educational policies and responses began to move towards integration. This was defined by Roy Jenkins as: 'not the flattening process of assimilation but an equal opportunity accompanied by cultural diversity in an atmosphere of mutual tolerance'.

Concern was expressed about the large numbers of Afro-Caribbean children in special schools. Most dispersal policies were also abandoned. What this meant was that schools began to recognise and value ethnic minority children's background, culture and language, to celebrate festivals, to organise multicultural and international evenings, and to use and teach mother tongues. There was also the beginning of Black Studies in some schools and teaching about ethnic history, art, music, religion and literature.

This idea of educational integration developed further into what is often called cultural pluralism. This was marked by educational strategies which many equate

with multiculturalism. The new idea was based upon the simple premise that society consisted of different groups and that education should reflect and value this diversity of lifestyles, beliefs and cultural traditions. This, it was held, would lead to all children responding more positively to the different beliefs, appearances and backgrounds of others.

This model barely had time to develop and establish itself clearly in terms of classroom practice before it met a rigorous challenge from the anti-racist lobby. At the beginning of the 1980s these educators argued forcefully that the multicultural response was wholly inadequate. It had been based, they declared, on a liberal belief that somehow knowledge and information could lead to a removal of racism and prejudice. They maintained that Britain was a racist society and that racism was more to do with the structure of that society than with individual attitudes. Clearly this was far removed from the early idea of assimilation which many had hoped would bring about a painless, gentle merging of native Britons and immigrant children.

Within this anti-racist model teachers should work towards the removal of all unjust structures and procedures. Educational strategies should ensure that a greater number of black people have power and influence. There should be more black and Asian headteachers, senior teachers, governors and education officers. All discrimination in the curriculum, classroom and school organisation should be removed.

This book is not intended to be a further chapter in the multicultural versus anti-racist debate. I believe enough time has been spent on choosing appropriate labels for teachers to work under. The danger has been that the debate has moved away from the classroom and into the world of academia.

In its booklet 'Multicultural & Anti-Racist Teaching Today', AMMA declares that 'Anti-racism seeks to cure and multicultural education to prevent the exercise of racial prejudice'. Neither of these positions can be wrong and both may be appropriate for different teachers and different schools at different times. The next section offers suggestions as to how the issues could begin to be raised in the staffroom. What is essential is that if one is using the term 'multicultural education', 'it must be defined at the outset of the discussion and the definition maintained throughout, the discussion otherwise becomes flabby and confused and its conclusion insecure'.
(Sir Keith Joseph 1985).

Most in-service courses about multicultural education follow this advice and begin with a session of definitions. One such exercise is outlined below.

Teachers are divided into small groups and given a statement and a number of possible responses. Their task is to put the responses in order of priority within

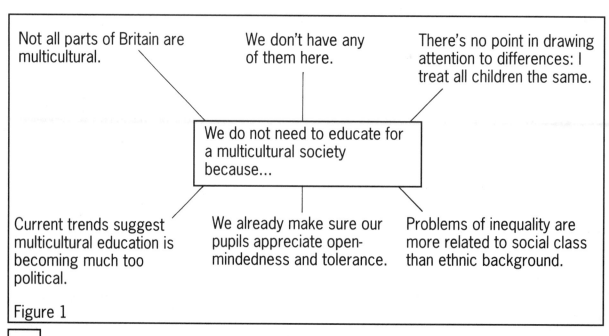

Not all parts of Britain are multicultural.

We don't have any of them here.

There's no point in drawing attention to differences: I treat all children the same.

We do not need to educate for a multicultural society because...

Current trends suggest multicultural education is becoming much too political.

We already make sure our pupils appreciate open-mindedness and tolerance.

Problems of inequality are more related to social class than ethnic background.

Figure 1

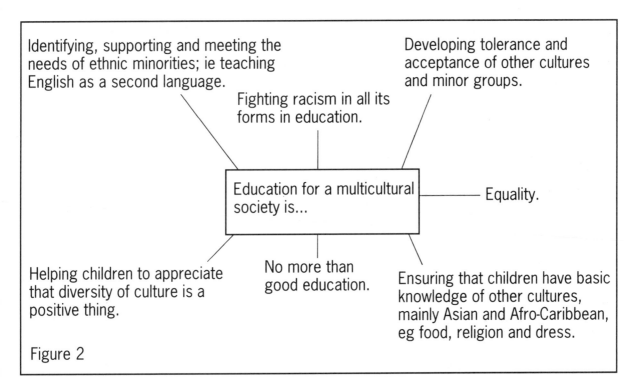

Identifying, supporting and meeting the needs of ethnic minorities; ie teaching English as a second language.

Fighting racism in all its forms in education.

Developing tolerance and acceptance of other cultures and minor groups.

Education for a multicultural society is...

Equality.

Helping children to appreciate that diversity of culture is a positive thing.

No more than good education.

Ensuring that children have basic knowledge of other cultures, mainly Asian and Afro-Caribbean, eg food, religion and dress.

Figure 2

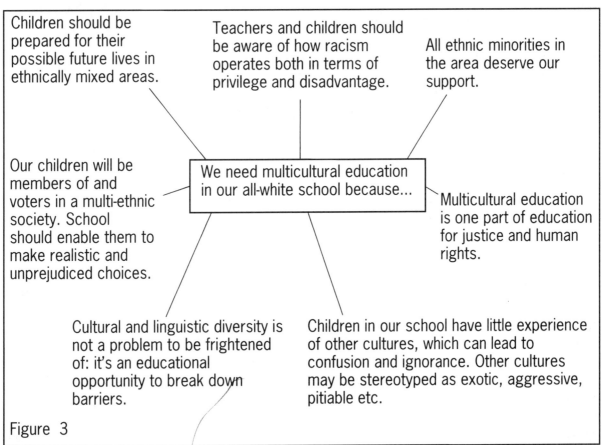

Children should be prepared for their possible future lives in ethnically mixed areas.

Teachers and children should be aware of how racism operates both in terms of privilege and disadvantage.

All ethnic minorities in the area deserve our support.

Our children will be members of and voters in a multi-ethnic society. School should enable them to make realistic and unprejudiced choices.

We need multicultural education in our all-white school because...

Multicultural education is one part of education for justice and human rights.

Cultural and linguistic diversity is not a problem to be frightened of: it's an educational opportunity to break down barriers.

Children in our school have little experience of other cultures, which can lead to confusion and ignorance. Other cultures may be stereotyped as exotic, aggressive, pitiable etc.

Figure 3

either their own educational philosophies or those of their school. The aim is to reach some understanding of the issues behind the label 'multicultural education'.

Possible statements and responses are given as Figures 1, 2 and 3.

Racism

Over the last ten years racism has become a central issue in any discussion about education for a multicultural society. The word has been used, overused and misused in many different ways and contexts. To many teachers it is full of political messages, innuendoes and threats. Many teachers cannot bring themselves even to use the word. These same people are often sympathetic to the responsibilities of education for promoting equal opportunities and a fairer society.

Why then the antipathy and hostility to the mention of anti-racism? Much of the blame must be attributed to the popular press which has created the stereotypical anti-racist, feminist, neo-Marxist, left wing councils who are 'using' education as a political tool to subvert the establishment. The result is that many teachers now equate both racism and anti-racism with political extremism. It is, however, also fair to say that the anti-racist position in education has been accompanied by much posturing and sloganising. Not enough has been offered to the classroom teacher.

However, the arguments cannot disguise the facts of racism in society, within schools and in the education system as a whole. There is, always has been, and probably always will be

prejudice against ethnic minorities. The experience of being the victim is not confined to Afro-Caribbean and Asian children. Italians, Jews and Irish people will testify to that.

Any discussion of education for a multicultural society must include discussion of racism. How do you raise the issue with teachers? It is almost certainly more likely to be accepted as an item on the agenda in the multi-ethnic school where few teachers can say they have not witnessed racism in some form. But what of the all-white school where direct manifestations of racism are perhaps less frequent? How do you persuade these teachers that racism and racial disadvantages should feature high in their priorities?

In my experience any INSET programme on multicultural education will always lead at some point to the subject of racism. This will often come from course members themselves. I would argue that this is more effective than so called 'racism awareness' courses, whose very title causes hackles to rise. How the discussion proceeds clearly depends upon the skill of the teacher trainer. I have included three activities which I have used successfully with groups of teachers.

Activity 1
Deciding on priority
The Swann Report 1985, *Education For All*, was much criticised for avoiding the subject of racism. The problem lay, however, in Lord Swann's summary, which was distributed to schools and was the only version most teachers had access to. This summary almost totally ignored Chapter Two of the main Swann Report. This chapter, 'Racism: Theory and Practice', is in fact a comprehensive

account of the issues and is well worth reading.

The activity that follows is based on this chapter. The extracts have been chosen to foster an initial discussion among teachers of issues such as stereotyping, the concept of prejudice, the influence of the media, and the roots of racism.

Divide the group into pairs and give each pair one of the statements below which are taken from Chapter Two of the Swann Report. Make sure that each pair is ready to respond to the statement and to share their response with the rest of the group.

After discussion, bring the group together. Each teacher should be given a full list of all statements. This means everyone has easy access to everybody else's statement.

Ask each pair to read their statement to the rest of the group.

Consider which statements are most important in any discussion of racism and try to put them in order of priority. Choose the nine most important statements and arrange them in a diamond shape as in Figure 4.

Statements for Activity 1
• 'It is almost as though having made use of workers who were prepared to work for lower wages and in worse conditions than indigenous workers at a time of apparent prosperity, the time has now come for them to "go back where they came from" since their services are no longer needed and they are seen as competing for jobs against indigenous workers.'
• 'Some of the stereotypes of certain ethnic minority groups can be seen as a legacy of history - from the days of the British Empire - and as a consequence of the view of other nations and peoples as in some sense "inferior", which was until

relatively recently promulgated through the curriculum offered by many schools.'
• 'In this respect we would see it as no more desirable or defensible for the education system to seek to create or perpetuate positive prejudices in favour of a particular group than to countenance negative views.'
• 'Prejudice thus requires that one has formed a stereotype of a particular "group" of people, be they women drivers, trade unionists or "immigrants", which then allows one to judge a mumber of this group, and in particular their actions, according to an established set of expectations.'
• 'Negative prejudice against ethnic minority groups can however extend beyond the "colour divide" and may be experienced, albeit to a lesser extent, by the "white" ethnic minorities in this country.'
• 'This was certainly true for the Vietnamese community ... where the initial wave of public goodwill towards the "boat people" has now been dissipated to a

High priority

Low priority

Figure 4

point where reports of racial harassment and attacks on Vietnamese families have sadly become more frequent.'

• 'One of the most vivid illustrations of how even long established ethnic minority communities can find themselves still regarded as "outsiders" is possibly the situation of the "black" community in Liverpool (and some other seaports in this country such as Cardiff and Bristol) which, although established over several generations, still suffer from extremes of racial prejudice.'

• '...that the education system can and must play a major part in challenging the stereotyping of ethnic minority communities in order to counter the pervasive influence of racism.'

• 'We could all be said to have "prejudices" in the sense of likes and dislikes and these are inevitably determined to a greater or lesser extent by our own upbringing and experiences, by the climate of opinion at the time, and by the facts or at least the version of them, however tenuous, that we receive from "influential others", be they family, friend, teacher, church-leader or the media.'

• '...those immigrants who came here for economic betterment and to enhance the prospects for their children came on the understanding that they had every right to come to this country.'

• '...to describe racism simply as a 'white' problem is similarly misconceived.'

Activity two
What happens in my school?
Racist behaviour can assume many forms. It can be direct or indirect, covert or overt, intentional or unintentional. This activity is intended to encourage teachers to question what happens in their own schools.

Work in pairs or groups and look at the following ways in which racism can manifest itself in a school setting. Tick those you can recognise as happening in your school. Which of them do you think is easiest to do something about? Which of them is hardest to do something about?

• Racist graffiti on the school buildings;
• Racist abuse directed at teachers, children, parents or ancillary staff;
• Name-calling;
• Defacing illustrations of black people in books;
• Racist attacks of a physical nature;
• Negative comments about black personalities;
• Negative comments about Third World or developing countries;
• School books which are out of date and present inaccurate or distorted views of the world;

- Racist jokes;
- Promulgation of myths about immigration;
- Use of books which fail to represent the multi-ethnic nature of British society.

Activity 3
What is racism?

Defining racism is not an easy task, and it is not necessarily a valuable activity. Many people equate racism with simple prejudice, while others view it as a cancer which runs through every aspect of education.

Asking teachers to reach a definition of racism can often result in formulae along the lines of the much quoted 'Racism equals Prejudice plus Power'. It is nonetheless important for teachers to share their own perceptions of prejudice, stereotyping and racism. Most teachers can accept the simple idea of prejudice, but not all forms of discriminatory behaviour are in fact caused by individual prejudice. This activity seeks to encourage teachers to look beyond such straightforward expressions of racism as verbal abuse or graffiti and to examine the wider definitions and implications. Read the following statements, each of which concerns an aspect of racism or racist behaviour. Try to think of two ways in which theory could be put into practice.

Statements for Activity 3
- 'We have, however, found some evidence of what we have described as unintentional racism in the behaviour and attitudes of teachers whom it would be misleading to describe as racist in the commonly accepted sense. They firmly believe that any prejudices they have can do no harm since they are not translated into open discriminatory practice. Nevertheless if their attitudes are influenced in any way by prejudices

against ethnic minority groups, this can and does, we believe, have a detrimental effect on all children whom they teach.' (Swann Report)

• 'Other forms of discrimination are less easy to perceive but are equally important. They include procedures employed within the education service, in its administration as well as in its institutions, which however well-intended or rooted in custom, may have the effect of reducing the opportunities open to members of ethnic minority groups.' (Draft policy statement on racism ILEA 1982)

• 'It is when this emotional prejudice extends to discriminatory behaviour that the result may merit the term 'racism'. For this to happen requires that the prejudiced person or group has to be in a position of sufficient power to extend discrimination. This is why, in Britain today, prejudice held by white people about black people is more dangerous in practice than the reverse prejudice.' (AMMA statement *Multicultural and Anti-Racist Education Today*)

Resources

Commonwealth Immigrants Advisory Committee (1964) 2nd Report (HMSO).
Multicultural and Anti-Racist Education Today: An AMMA Statement. This offers a useful examination of most of the issues, including language, the curriculum, examinations and anti-racist strategies.
Education for All, Swann Report (HMSO).
Black Settlers in Britain 1555-1958, Nigel File and Chris Power (Heinemann). This provides some extremely useful material for middle and junior children.
Staying Power - the History of Black People in Britain, Peter Fryer (Pluto Press). An exhaustive but readable account for teacher reference.
Black People in Britain 1650-1850, Tessa Hosking (Macmillan). This book examines why black people came to Britain between 1650 and 1850, what they did and what contemporary attitudes were.
Lascars and Princes - the History of Indian People in Britain, 1700-1947, R Visram (Pluto Press). This is an extremely readable account of the Indian presence in Britain, for teacher reference.

Chapter Two

A multicultural curriculum

'What multicultural aspects do you include in your curriculum?'

'You've taken account of the LEA's multicultural policy, haven't you?'

Questions of this kind often cause great difficulty and soul-searching in school planning sessions and meetings.

Many teachers in all-white schools are apprehensive when the multicultural curriculum is mentioned. There are usually two reasons. Firstly they do not see what relevance it has to their school; they believe that multicultural education belongs only in schools with a high percentage of ethnic minority pupils. By 'ethnic minority' they mean Asian or Afro-Caribbean. The first chapter, I hope, has dealt adequately with this misconception,

but it would perhaps be worthwhile to re-affirm that, in the words of *Our Multicultural Society: The Educational Response* (AMMA 1983): 'Pupils from all backgrounds will one day be voting, decision-making citizens whose views will influence public policies which affect people from all cultural backgrounds. All will contribute to the values of society. It is therefore important that all are made aware of the multicultural nature of British society today and are encouraged in the attitudes of mutual knowledge, understanding and tolerance which alone can make such a multicultural society a fair and successful one'.

The second major reason for apprehension about a multicultural

curriculum is the fear that it will somehow lead to the neglect of basic skills in favour of more peripheral activities. There is also a fear that there will not be enough time to do other more important things. In fact the reverse is true. The multicultural curriculum is often, perhaps rather glibly, described as being 'nothing more than good education'. It follows that the curriculum is incomplete without some consideration of a multicultural dimension.

The reasons for misgivings and misconceptions about the multicultural curriculum can be traced back to educational responses in the 1960s. The arrival of large numbers of children who did not speak English meant that a specific educational need was clearly identified. The need was met with large doses of English as a second language.

Because almost the only educational response was concerned with 'doing something about those children', it was perhaps not surprising that multicultural education became equated with multi-ethnic schools and 'those' children.

As we have observed in Chapter One, this model of provision was questioned in the late 1960s and early 1970s, and two priorities emerged:
• Meeting the educational needs of ethnic minority pupils.
• Broadening the education offered to all pupils to reflect the multiracial nature of British society.

At this point interest moved to curriculum content and the development of positive attitudes towards both self and others.

However, this second aim of broadening the education offered to all pupils has not been easy to achieve. Key words throughout any debate of this area include 'tokenism', 'permeation', 'multicultural' and 'anti-racist'.

Early attempts to develop a multicultural curriculum often took the form of adding some element on to the existing curriculum or setting multicultural education within certain subject areas like humanities or social studies. The problem with this approach was that the very issues with which it purported to deal were pushed into one small area rather than being seen as central to the whole curriculum.

Current thinking strongly favours permeation. Multicultural education is not just another subject in the curriculum. It is not to be seen as a separate element but rather as a dimension or perspective, whether the focus is on mathematics, science or humanities.

The expression 'tokenism' has been much used in describing some efforts in

curriculum development. It has been used to deride and belittle the efforts of the so-called 'steel band, sari and samosa' type. Through tokenism, multicultural education has sometimes become an exotic or spectacular element. This takes a variety of forms: the one-off celebration of Diwali (perhaps at the wrong time of the year), the exotic food-tasting sessions or the international evening. Any development along these lines, if it is a school's total response to a multicultural society, is wholly inadequate. However, many schools have little idea about a multicultural curriculum and are simply unsure about where and how to start. There is little point in belittling genuine innovations, and of course there is a place for this sort of highlight within the school curriculum, when it arises naturally.

Perhaps it would be fairer to look at these 'tokenistic' efforts as small steps along a long road. In my experience most schools have gone through a number of stages of development, all of which have contributed to the learning process. The first stage will almost certainly comprise small-scale innovations. They are not small-scale in terms of their worth but rather limited in their application throughout the rest of the curriculum.

Multi-faith religious education has been a favourite place to begin. These small steps are often dependent upon the enthusiasm and expertise of either an individual teacher or perhaps a year team. These teachers will probably be working in isolation and facing apathy, incomprehension, accusations of jumping on the bandwagon, or even open hostility from other members of staff.

The next stage is for these small-scale innovations to be seen as a part of the broad curriculum framework of the school, following on from the premise that multicultural perspectives should permeate every aspect of the curriculum. This is a time for the whole staff to consider their response. It is not an easy stage, and it needs to be considered carefully within the school's INSET programme and development plan. The school should, however, be asking itself questions along the lines of the following extract from the ILEA document, *Education in a Multi-ethnic Society: An Aide-memoire to the Inspectorate.*

School policy

In what ways has the school responded to the ILEA policy statements and position papers on multi-ethnic education?

How far is the school integrating multi-ethnic policies and practices into its overall framework of operation?

Equality of opportunity

Does the school demonstrate, in its organisation and in what it offers to pupils, an understanding of the complexities and subtleties of providing for equality of opportunity?

Racism

Have the damaging effects on pupils' lives of all forms of racism been examined by staff in order to formulate a school policy?

Is the school developing strategies for opposing racism within the curriculum and through extra-curricular activities and counselling?

Curriculum

To what extent does the curriculum reflect, in its stated objectives and in its content and activities, that our society is multi-ethnic?

Classroom strategies

Are teachers aware of the role they play in creating an atmosphere and in using methods which encourage pupils from a range of cultural backgrounds to work together?

Resources

Do the school's resources reflect the needs of pupils learning in a multi-ethnic society? Is the full range of cultures within society represented in the school's resources?

Language

Are staff knowledgeable about the linguistic 'repertoires' of their pupils? Are special needs - for example, to learn English as a second language - being met? Is the validity of pupils' dialects recognised in the language work of the school?

Ethos and atmosphere

Does the school actively seek to promote the positive value of our multi-ethnic society?

How is this shown in the attitudes of the pupils, in the curricular and extra-curricular programmes developed by the school, and in the resources used to support these activities?

Aspects for review

Let us return to the premise that multicultural education is simply good education, and look more closely at this statement through a basic INSET activity.

Working in groups, teachers were given an envelope containing a number of statements outlining the objectives for multicultural education. These were based on Jeffcoate's model in *The School in the Multicultural Society* (1986). The statements had been mixed up and teachers were asked to sort them out under three headings: knowledge, skills and attitudes.

Respect for others

Knowledge
Children should know the fundamental facts of race and racial differences:
• the different beliefs and customs of the main cultures represented in Britain on both a national and local level;
• the reasons which have brought the different groups to Britain, and specifically factors determining the ethnic composition of the local area.

Skills

All pupils should be able to:
• distinguish fact from opinion and assess the factual content in what they see, hear or read;
• be dispassionate about their own cultures.

Attitudes

All pupils should accept:
• that every human being is unique;
• that we share a common humanity;
• that equal rights and justice are the right of all people;
• that the achievements of other cultures and nations are of value;
• the presence of strangers without feeling threatened;
• that Britain is composed of people of many races;
• that no culture is ever static and that all

groups within a growing multicultural society will have to evolve and adapt to each other;
• that prejudice and discrimination are common in our society for specific reasons, both social and historic;
• the damaging effect of prejudice and discrimination;
• that it is possible to develop multiple loyalties.

Respect for self

Knowledge
All pupils should know:
• what is distinctive and special about the history and achievements of their own culture.

Skills

All pupils should be able to:
• communicate clearly in English and in their own mother tongue if this is not English.

Attitudes

All pupils should have developed:
• a good self-image;
• a strong and positive sense of their own identities.
  Once the sorting out activity was completed teachers were asked to compare their choices with the DES document (1981) which outlined the six central aims of the school curriculum as listed below:
1 To help pupils to develop lively, enquiring minds, the ability to question and argue rationally and to apply themselves to tasks and physical skills.
2 To help pupils to acquire knowledge and skills relevant to adult life and employment in a fast-changing world.

3 To help pupils to use language and number effectively.

4 To instil respect for religious and moral values and tolerance for other races, religions and ways of life.

5 To help pupils to understand the world in which they live and the interdependence of individuals, groups and nations.

6 To help to appreciate human achievements and aspirations.

What emerges from any follow-up discussion is that the two documents are very similar in their objectives and that far from being a tag-on, multicultural education is indistinguishable from central curriculum aims.

The difficulty often lies in taking teachers beyond the initial narrow perception of multicultural education as something that is really only for 'those' schools with a large number of 'those'

children! It can also be difficult to take teachers beyond that equally restricting second image, that when multicultural education appears within the curriculum of an all-white school it will still be about 'those' children.

So what is appropriate to the multicultural curriculum? Teaching children about other cultures will not per se have any effect upon attitudes to those cultures, whether positive or negative. Multicultural education is not simply learning about Asian and Afro-Caribbean children; it draws educational experiences from a diversity of cultures, both within Britain and world-wide.

There can be few arguments against multicultural education when teachers have been offered its wider unchallengeable definition. Who can argue that the curriculum should not encourage

consideration of the concepts of fairness, co-operation, conflict, power, interdependence, similarity and differences, justice, tradition, values and beliefs? It cannot be denied that the curriculum should encourage:

• Interest in the immediate and world community;
• An open mind;
• A positive self-image;
• Tolerance towards other people irrespective of race, gender, disability or class;
• A desire to see change for the better;
• Respect for our own and other people's lifestyles;
• An understanding of the need to co-operate and work together.

Likewise it cannot be denied that the curriculum should encourage development of the following skills:

• co-operation;
• problem solving;
• decision making;
• prediction;
• drawing conclusions;
• social skills;
• critical skills;
• communication.

Aspects of the multicultural curriculum

If we accept the much broader definition of multicultural education, how will it shape the curriculum? Firstly it is much easier to see multicultural education as a process which permeates the curriculum, rather than something which is added on

as an afterthought or which looks only at the strange and exotic.

Secondly it is much easier for teachers to consider multicultural education as an essential perspective for any theme or subject if they understand that it does not always need to refer directly to Britain's multi-racial society. It is clearly more useful to aim at developing attitudes of justice, tolerance and respect than to introduce contrived references to the Asian and Afro-Caribbean communities. Certain themes and subject areas lend themselves readily to multicultural perspectives. In others the link may be less obvious. Chapters Six and Seven will look in detail at planning and developing possible themes, but we shall briefly examine this now.

Examples of themes drawing content directly from Britain's multicultural society are Festivals, Celebrations, Myself, Food,

Stories, On The Move, Families. Other less 'direct' themes may include Water, Rainforests, The Media, and Arctic People.

A class working on celebrations might look at past and present celebrations, both within the community and world-wide. A class working on the topic of water may look at the issue of safe and unsafe water, asking, for example, 'Why does 51 per cent of the world still not have safe water?'. Within both these themes there is ample scope to develop and foster those attitudes of respect and tolerance for our own and other people's lifestyles, as well as a desire to see a fairer world and an awareness of how our attitudes are shaped by many influences.

Some specific subject areas appear at first glance to offer limited opportunities for multicultural content. For example, it is easier for policy documents to talk of multicultural perspectives permeating mathematics than it is to offer practical examples of what the teacher can do in the classroom. Children undertake a lot of mathematics work between the ages of five and 16. If we acknowledge that all subject areas should aim to develop co-operation, collaboration, positive self-image, and working together in a fair and just manner, then these subject areas are probably making their contribution.

National Curriculum

The implementation of the National Curriculum as laid down in the Education Reform Act 1988 has been seen by some as restricting multicultural education, in that issues relating to equal opportunity and injustice will be pushed to one side.

On the other hand it has been argued that ERA could be an ideal opportunity for all schools to re-appraise their classroom organisation, methodology and curriculum.

In considering the foundation subjects of the National Curriculum I shall refer to such specific documents as are available at the time of writing. It is useful to look at the general document *National Curriculum: From Policy into Practice* (DES 1989), and see what this has to offer in the context of multicultural education.

From Policy into Practice (the red document) deals with 'the curriculum for pupils of compulsory school age, and the new legal requirements for that curriculum contained in the Education Reform Act 1988 (ERA)'. It aims to set the National Curriculum in context and to show how the ERA requirements relate to thinking about the curriculum over the last two decades. It also explains how the National Curriculum and related requirements will affect practice in schools.

The booklet has been distributed to all maintained school teachers and student teachers and is designed as a guide. What then of multicultural education? What will the teacher in an all-white primary school think on reading through the document? Will they be any more convinced that multicultural education is education for all?

From Policy into Practice 2.1 looks at the first section of the ERA and the general principles which must be reflected in the curriculum. This first section of the ERA entitles all pupils to a curriculum which:

• 'promotes the spiritual, moral, cultural, mental and physical development of pupils at the school, and of society;'
• 'prepares such pupils for the opportunities, responsibilities and experiences of adult life.'

From Policy into Practice 2.2 considers the implications of these for the curriculum and includes the following:

'The curriculum must also serve to develop the pupil as an individual, as a member of society and as a future adult member of the community with a range of personal and social opportunities and responsibilities.'

The words 'spiritual' and 'moral' must surely imply consideration of justice and inequality, and racism in particular. 'Preparing pupils for adult life' and 'as a member of society' must imply consideration of what that society is.

Section 3 of *From Policy into Practice* outlines the National Curriculum. It is here that we can find direct support for multicultural education. It is worth quoting the whole section.

'The foundation subjects are certainly not a complete curriculum; they are necessary but not sufficient to ensure a curriculum which meets the purposes and covers the elements identified by HMI and others. In particular, they will cover fully the acquisition of certain key cross-curricular competences; literacy, numeracy and information technology skills. More will, however, be needed to secure the kind of curriculum required by section 1 of the ERA. The whole curriculum for all pupils will certainly need to include at appropriate (and in some cases all) stages:
a) careers education and guidance;
b) health education;
c) other aspects of personal and social education; and
d) coverage across the curriculum of gender and multicultural issues.

'These areas of the curriculum are not separately indentified as part of the statutory National Curriculum because all the requirements associated with

foundation subjects could not appropriately be applied to them in all respects. But they are clearly required in the curriculum which all pupils are entitled to by virtue of Section 1 of the Act. A great deal of learning related to these themes can and should be covered for all pupils in the context of the foundation subjects, and some elements will certainly be contained in the attainment targets and programmes of study.'

At first glance this section seems to offer a green light for multicultural issues. It appears that if any of the four elements identified above, including 'coverage across the curriculum of gender and multicultural issues', is not identifiable within the National Curriculum, then the curricular requirements as laid down in Section 1 of the Act are not being met. To see this as a legal requirement for schools to deliver a National 'multicultural' Curriculum is perhaps naive and over-optimistic. It is nevertheless encouraging to find reference to multicultural issues in a prominent place within the guidelines being offered to schools.

Resources

Education in a Multi-ethnic Society: An Aide-memoire to the Inspectorate (ILEA 1981).

National Curriculum *From Policy into Practice* (DES 1989).

The School in the Multicultural Society, James and Jeffcoate (eds) 1986 (Paul Chapman Publishing).

Multicultural Education: Principles and Practice, Lynch (Routledge).

A Teacher's Guide to Multicultural Education, Nixon (Basil Blackwell).

Chapter Three

Core subjects

The National Curriculum, as defined in the ERA, comprises:

• Foundation subjects, including three core subjects and seven other foundation subjects which must be included in the curricula of all pupils;

• Attainment targets to be specified at up to ten levels of attainment covering the ages five to 16, setting objectives for learning;

• Programmes of study specifying essential teaching within each subject area;

• Assessment arrangements related to the ten levels of attainment.

ERA is very clear that it does not require teaching to be provided under the specific subject headings. It follows then that much of the teaching for the foundation subjects will continue to take place in cross-curricular contexts, often within a particular theme or topic.

This chapter will look at the three core elements, English, maths and science, and examine ways in which multicultural perspectives can be developed in these areas.

Although it is possible to identify certain specific areas and activities for the three core subjects, it must be emphasised that many activities will take place across the curriculum.

English

English is a subject area which seems to give many opportunities for multicultural perspectives, both in the choice of literature offered to children and through the medium of discussion. However, the outcome often seems to be that other subject departments identify multiculturalism solely with English. Within the primary school, though, language development is a priority, and this of course takes place across the curriculum.

This section begins by looking at the proposals in the *National Curriculum for English 5-11*. What support for multicultural education, if any, is evident in the documents published so far?

The proposals for English between the ages of five to eleven were contained within a consultative document, variously labelled *The Cox Report* or 'the yellow document'.

The consultative document

It was extremely encouraging to find many references to multicultural issues throughout *The Cox Report*. The report considered, among other things, the specific needs of bilingual learners, language varieties and change, dialects, writing systems and literature.

It is clear that these considerations influenced the thinking of the committee. This is, of course, heartening; but it could also be further evidence of the misconception that multiculturalism is a natural part of English while other subject areas have little part to play. This will become more apparent when we consider the National Curriculum material available in science and maths.

The key references in *The Cox Report* are outlined below. The suggestions fall outside the proposed attainment targets but they are clearly intended to help in meeting them. It would be hoped that they would be of great significance for any school considering its language policy.

From Chapter Three, 'English in the National Curriculum':

3.6 A statement of the aims of English teaching also makes it easier to relate the use of English and knowledge about it to the wider area of language in general. It is not within our brief to make recommendations about the teaching of other languages. However, as the Bullock Report clearly stated in 1975: 'No child should be expected to cast off the language and culture of the home as he [or she] crosses the school threshold, and the curriculum should reflect this'.

3.7 A major assumption which we are making is that the curriculum for all pupils should include informed discussion of the multicultural nature of British society, whether or not the individual school is culturally mixed. It is essential that the development of competence in spoken and written Standard English is sensitive to the knowledge of other languages which many children have. As well as the many different mother tongues that are present in our multicultural, multilingual society, there are also the foreign languages that are taught in schools. A rich source of insight into the nature of language is lost if English is treated in complete isolation.

3.11 Teachers should accordingly be encouraged to develop whole school policies on language, which are sensitive to their local circumstances, and which meet the objective that when children leave school they should have acquired as far as is possible:

• a firmly based, but flexible and developing, linguistic and cultural identity;

• an awareness of some of the basic properties of human languages and their role in societies;

• a respect for other languages and cultures; and an understanding of the increasing interaction of cultures in society;

• a willingness and capability to overcome communication barriers.

From Chapter Five - 'Linguistic Terminology':

5.38 Variety in language arises because language changes according to topic, addressee, the formality of the setting, the nature of the task. It also changes over historical time, in different geographical regions, and in different social groups, defined by ethnicity, class, gender, and so on. The main concept, which goes against much traditional thinking about language, is that such change is a natural and inevitable process. (Resistance to this idea could be illustrated in detail from newspaper commentary on linguistic matters.)

5.40 Terms of the following kinds are likely to be needed:

• *formal language, casual or colloquial language, slang;*

• *first language, second language, foreign language;*

• *accent, dialect, creole, international language, lingua franca;*

• *historical, geographical and social dialects.*

From Chapter Six - 'Literature':

6.1 In this active involvement with literature pupils gain more lives than their own. They will encounter and come to understand a wider range of feelings and relationships by vicariously entering the worlds of others, and in consequence they are likely to understand more of themselves.

6.3 Programmes of study in literature should encourage pupils to enjoy a wide range of literary forms. Children should be introduced to both 20th and pre-20th century literature, to literature from the constituent countries of the British Isles, of the Commonwealth, and of the wide English-speaking world. Today literature in English in the classroom can be drawn from many different countries; children need to be aware of the richness of contemporary writing, so that they may be introduced to the ideas and feelings of people from cultures different from their own.

In addition, Chapter Six offered a list of authors to consider. Those with 'multicultural' sympathies include: Janet and Allan Ahlberg, Bernard Ashley, Petronella Breinburg, Babette Cole, Marjorie Darke, Anita Desai, Faroukh Dhondy, Shirley Hughes, Geraldine Kaye, Gene Kemp, Robert Leeson, Joan Lingard, Jan Ormerod, Helen Oxenbury and Michael Rosen.

Finally, Chapter Twelve was devoted to the issues of bilingual children.

It is apparent, then, that the multicultural perspective is seen as an essential element within the proposals for English between five and eleven. The next part of this chapter will offer suggestions for developing this. Most schools and teachers will hopefully avoid teaching solely around the attainment targets. The curriculum should continue to reflect the needs of the child rather than the form of assessment.

I have chosen a number of areas and activities which offer multicultural opportunities within the scope of language development.

Using photographs

I have found that the use of photographs can be a challenging and entertaining activity, full of potential for language work. The advantages of using photographs as an aid to developing multicultural perspectives include:
• Presenting positive images of minority groups within our society;
• Challenging preconceived images of people and issues;
• Presenting pictures of Britain and the world as it really is;
• Encouraging children to be aware of detail within photographs;
• Encouraging children to look beyond the obvious;
• Encouraging children to have a positive self-image;
• Developing an awareness of bias;
• Raising issues of race, gender and disability;
• Offering information other than through the printed word;
• Encouraging group work, co-operation and collaboration.
Using photographs also supports and develops numerous language skills. These include:
• Talking in a casual context;
• Responding to visual stimuli;
• Listening to and telling unscripted stories;
• Sharing experiences;
• Asking and answering questions;
• Giving and receiving simple explanations;
• Arguing a point of view;
• Expressing opinions;
• Predicting outcomes and possibilities.

There are many different ways to use photographs. You might use them as a starting point for a theme, or to support a topic. What is offered below is only a selection, capable of much variation. I believe the use of photographs is a perfect illustration of the idea that multicultural teaching is being no more than good education.

All the activities have clear implications for classroom management. There is little point in setting up an activity if not all children can see the photographs, or if the photographs are too small or of poor quality.

Kim's game

Put a number of large photographs on the wall or blackboard. Let the children have a set time to look at them individually, in pairs or in groups. Cover the photographs with a large sheet of paper and ask the children to write down or talk about as many as they can remember.

Alternatively children could be asked more precise questions. Which photographs were in the bottom row? Which photographs were in the corners?

Even this basic activity can raise questions of language. What words do the children choose to describe Afro-Caribbean or Asian children or people with disabilities?

The teacher must be ready to respond to negative comments and be sure of her own use of language.

Which one's gone?

Put a selection of large photographs on the wall or blackboard. Allow the children some time to look at them. Ask the children to close their eyes or put their heads on the desk while you take one photograph away. Ask the children which one is missing. This can be varied by taking two, three or more away.

How many people?

Display a selection of large photographs. Ask the children to look at the people in them. How many children are there? How many adults? How many disabled people? How many girls? How many Afro-Caribbean people? How many white people? Questions like this can lead on to issues such as the accuracy of representation within the media. Children could do their own research in newspapers, analysing the number of photographs depicting ethnic minorities. They could then be encouraged to write to the editors for a response to their findings.

Describe and draw

Divide the class into small groups and give one child in each group a photograph. Ask her to describe it as accurately as possible to the others who then try to draw it. This is an excellent activity to encourage questioning, describing and listening skills.

Connections

Put a selection of photographs up on the wall or blackboard, turned face inwards. Ask a child to turn two over at random, then make a connection between the two. This can be any connection, such as 'There are animals in both' or 'There are girls in both'.

Obviously the teacher controls the situation in his choice of photographs. The activity can be varied by increasing the number of photographs, or by specifying in advance the type of connection to be made.

Categorising

Give groups or pairs of children a number of photographs and ask them to sort and classify them under a number of headings. The level of difficulty depends on the age of the children. Younger children can be asked to sort very specifically. Older children could be given a selection of photos and asked to devise ways to categorise them.

It's your choice

This is an excellent activity for introducing issues in an interesting and challenging manner. Display about 20 photographs around the room. Under each photograph fix a piece of A4 paper. Give each child up to four coloured stickers on which they write their name or initials. Ask them to look at the photographs around the room and put their stickers on the ones they like best, find most unusual or would most like to be in. The criteria for selection depends on the direction the teacher wishes to take.

Once they have made their individual choices, ask the children to give reasons for their choices. Repeat the exercise with the children working in pairs. This raises interesting questions for working together. They will have to listen to each other and, hopefully, collaborate and compromise.

Once the pairs have made their choices, ask them to return to their places and look around at the overall selection.

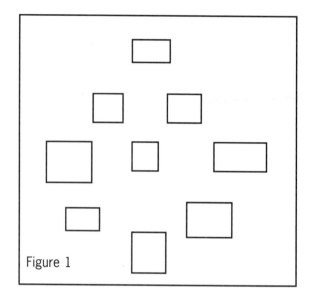

Figure 1

Interesting questions will inevitably arise, such as 'Why did everyone think the man ironing was an unusual picture?' or 'Why did no-one choose the black family as a happy one?'. Ask the children how they arrived at their compromise.

Ranking exercise

Give the children a number of photographs and a large piece of paper. Mark the paper beforehand with the priority pattern you wish to achieve as in Figure 1, or some such variation. Ask the children to rank the photographs according to whatever criteria you choose, such as 'the photograph you like best goes at the top, the one you like least at the bottom'. Other criteria might be 'most interesting', 'most unusual', 'happiest', 'the one you would like to be in' or 'the one you would like to do'.

Making questions

Choose one large photograph and put it on the blackboard. Tell the children that there are a number of questions you would like them to answer concerning the photograph. Write these questions on card beforehand and place them on the board one at a time. The questions do not have to be difficult or complicated. Within any photograph there will be countless possibilities. Ask them to try to answer the question.

Give each group a photograph, a large sheet of paper and some adhesive. Place the photograph in the centre of the paper and divide the rest of the sheet into two, four or six sections. Allocate each child a space to write a large question concerning the photograph. Once completed, pass each piece of paper to the next group and ask them to answer the questions while their own are answered by another group.

Options

Give the children a number of photographs and a selection of captions. Ask them to choose the most appropriate captions for each photograph, or alternatively to write some of their own.

Which photographs to use?

Taking your own photographs in a school or community setting provides you with a resource that the children can immediately recognise and identify with. In addition there are numerous photosets available which have been specifically designed to raise issues related to multicultural education. Questions of development and global education, human rights, ethnic minorities in Britain, gender, disability and religion can all be covered.

What is a family?

This photoset contains 24 black and white photographs about families in Britain.

There is also an excellent teachers' book which is full of practical suggestions for activities based on the photographs.

The set raises issues of stereotyping in terms of race, gender or handicap within the family, asking questions about marriage, divorce, roles and relationships. The introduction makes it clear that the aim of the pack is to raise consciousness without devaluing individual points of view; not to change people's minds but to make them aware of other possibilities.

The set is available from the Development Education Centre, Birmingham.

Behind the scenes

This photoset contains 24 black and white photographs. There is a useful teachers' book suggesting many activities. The set is designed for use in school-based in-service to raise issues around the 'hidden curriculum'. The photographs show varied scenes in primary schools and suggest issues of race, gender and parental involvement. The set is available from the Development Education Centre, Birmingham.

Tale of two cities: Calcutta and London

This is a collection of 64 large black and white photographs which sets out to challenge our images and perceptions of life in Calcutta and London. It covers themes such as transport, work, education and homelessness. Each photograph of London is juxtaposed with one from Calcutta on the same theme. All kinds of questions are raised about similarities and differences in lifestyles. There is wealth in both Calcutta and London; there is also homelessness and begging in both. This is an excellent and important collection of photographs. It is available from the World Wide Fund for Nature.

Images

This is a set of 24 photographs from Britain and Africa. It contains suggestions for a complete unit of work around the photographs. Although the pack was designed for GCSE I have used it successfully with top junior children. The photographs have been selected to offer a positive image of Africa, and to develop in children an awareness of how false and inaccurate images arise. The pack raises 'issues of stereotyping based on class, race and gender'. It is available from Action Aid.

Weddings

This is a set of 15 A3 full colour photographs depicting scenes from Hindu, Moslem, Sikh, Jewish, Christian and Chinese wedding ceremonies. There is a thorough teacher's guide with details of the history, ritual and clothing. The set is available from E J Arnold and Son.

Festival food

This set contains six A3 full-colour photographs illustrating typical dishes served at the following religious festivals: Eid, Diwali, Passover, Christmas, Easter, Chinese New Year and Dragon Boat Festival. It is available from E J Arnold and Son.

Religious services

This is a set of 12 full colour photographs depicting six different religions - Christian, Moslem, Sikh, Hindu, Buddhist and Jewish. The photographs show the place of worship and a service in progress, and are available from E J Arnold and Son.

Food

This pack consists of 31 photographs, with detailed teachers' notes. Four main themes are presented: Shops, Eating, Preparation and Restaurants. The set draws on a number of different cultures. It is available from Galt Educational.

Using fiction

Multicultural fiction is simply fiction that can offer support to a number of perspectives. It is important that libraries and classrooms do not establish 'multicultural' corners, where there is often an ornate display of the evidence. There might be occasions when a number of books are displayed for a purpose, but a permanent section is not to be recommended. 'Multicultural' fiction is fiction that stands in its own right.

Chapter Five will look at some criteria which have been suggested for use when choosing books and other learning materials. In this section I intend to offer a selection of those books which support the aims of multicultural education within its broadest definition. These books might:
• Raise issues, like apartheid or human rights. Books like this are concerned with specific issues and can form the basis for cross-curricular work.
• Use folk tales to demonstrate the commonality of human experience, showing how people share the same experience and emotions; or to illustrate stories that have travelled and explain why.
• Contain stories about contemporary

Britain in which people from minorities play important positive roles rather than just being included as exotic names and stereotypes.

• Have illustrations that acknowledge the presence of black and Asian people and other minorities in British society. These would offer children in all schools a window on the wider world.

• Be dual-language books. Many people imagine these books only have a role in classrooms where there are a number of bilingual children. They can, however, be useful in the monolingual classroom, for example, in showing children that there are writing systems other than Roman script. Dual-language books can be used to reinforce the value of other languages, showing that they are not merely a collection of 'strange' sounds and symbols but that they can tell exactly the same story as the English version. There is an increasing number of titles with a multicultural perspective which are suitable for the classroom or library. The two lists below are simply personal favourites which have been tried and tested in schools.

For four- to eight-year-olds

Say it Again, Granny, John Agard (Mammoth Paperbacks). This is a delightful collection of 20 poems based on Caribbean proverbs. It is marvellously written and sensitively illustrated. It would be suitable for top infants.

Abiyoyo, Pete Seeger (Hamish Hamilton). This tale of a people-eating monster is adapted from an old South African folk tale. It contains important messages about people living together but above all is fun! It is suitable for top infants.

Flossie and the Fox, Patricia C McKissack (Viking Kestrel). This is a very well illustrated story of a little black girl in the American South who meets and outsmarts a crafty fox intent on stealing her basket of eggs. It is suitable for top infants.

The Big Alfie and Annie Rose Storybook, Shirley Hughes (The Bodley Head). This is a collection of stories and poems featuring Alfie and his little sister. Shirley Hughes' detailed illustrations are always a reminder of multiracial Britain. The book includes the story 'Here comes the Bridesmaid', set around the wedding of an Afro-Caribbean couple. It is suitable for children from four upwards.

Not So Fast, Songololo, Niki Daly (Gollancz). This is a tale of Shepherd, a small South African boy who likes doing things slowly. It has colourful illustrations and an attractively written text. It is suitable for top infants.

The Baby's Catalogue, Allan and Janet Ahlberg (Viking Kestrel). This is a marvellous account in pictures of the life of six babies in five families. One of the families is black and other illustrations show non-stereotyped roles. It is sure to be a favourite for years to come. It is ideal for babies and children.

Ten, Nine, Eight, Molly Bang (Picture Puffin). This is an early counting book set around bedtime. There are marvellous, clear illustrations reflecting the obviously close relationship of a little black girl and her father. It is a useful first and pre-reader.

Ming's Surprise, Ling's New Year, Winston's Roller Skates, Winklet's New Coat and *Winklet Goes to School*, Eileen Ryder (Burke Books). This is an attractive set of stories featuring children from a variety of ethnic backgrounds. Each story is simply told and attractively illustrated. They are suitable for younger infants.

My Brother Sean, Petronella Breinburg

(Bodley Head). This is an excellent story for younger children. They have clear positive illustrations of familiar situations.

For eight- to twelve-year-olds

Come on into my Tropical Garden, Grace Nichols (A & C Black). This is a collection of poems which 'evoke the Caribbean, its people, its sounds and tastes'. The black and white illustrations are beautifully detailed.

The Julian Stories, Ann Cameron (Gollancz). These six stories of Julian and his little brother Huey and their relationship with their father are full of humour and enjoyment.

Listen to this Story, Grace Hallworth (Magnet). This delightful collection of stories is inspired by the customs, folklore and humour of the Caribbean islands.

That'd be Telling, compiled by Michael Rosen and Joan Griffiths (Cambridge Educational). This anthology is a collection of stories from a wide range of cultural traditions together with a number of songs and riddles. It is based on the successful BBC schools radio series. A cassette of selected stories and songs is available.

The Village by the Sea, Anita Desai (Puffin Plus). This book is set in India and its theme is the harsh realities of life in city and village. It tells the story of Hari and his sister Lila and their struggle to hold their family together. The book is also available in cassette form from Mantra books. It is suitable for 11-12 year-olds.

The Conker as Hard as a Diamond, Chris Powling (Kestrel Kites). This is an amusing story of a magical conker which features Alpesh, an Asian child, as the main character. It is suitable for lower juniors.

I Like That Stuff - Poems from Many Cultures, Morag Styles (Cambridge University Press). This is an excellent wide-ranging anthology of poems from many different cultures for eight- to twelve-year-olds.

I'm Trying to Tell You, Bernard Ashley (Puffin). Nerissa, Ray, Lyn and Prakash are all in the same class at Saffin Street School but each of them has a different story to tell.

The Devil's Children, Peter Dickinson (Puffin). This is the first in Peter

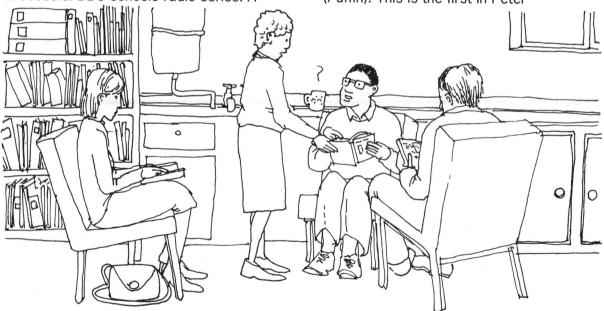

Dickinson's futuristic trilogy, *Changes*. This book focuses on a young white girl's relationship with a group of Sikhs who are unaffected by the madness gripping Britain. The book examines prejudice and fear born of ignorance. It is suitable for older juniors.

Visitors to school and classroom

Involving children in the experience of preparing for and meeting a visitor can be a rich source of pleasure and interest and give many opportunities for language work. There should be many chances to develop skills across different language levels:
- casual talk;
- responses to visual and aural stimuli;
- listening to and telling unscripted stories;
- sharing experiences;
- answering and asking questions;
- interviewing;
- giving and receiving explanations and information;
- letter-writing.

There can be scope for positive experiences of different lifestyles including language, religion, clothing, food etc. For some children it might be their first opportunity to meet with people from a minority group or to talk to a person with a different coloured skin. The children will bring their own preconceived ideas and, certainly, at an older level, prejudices.

There are many possible pitfalls, and the main message is one of sensitivity, awareness and, above all, preparation. Obviously a teacher would not intend to present the visitor as an example of an exotic food habit, funny religion or simply different coloured skin, but the effect can be just that if the session is not carefully thought out beforehand. There are a

number of factors that ought to be considered.

Why use a visitor?

It is probable that your visitor will have been invited into the classroom to support a specific topic that the children have been working on. In this way there will be opportunities to extend and enrich the children's learning, to develop social and language skills, and for the children to share what they have learnt so far. In addition the visitor will provide the children with the chance to develop positive attitudes towards other people. A visitor from an ethnic minority might offer a child his first opportunity to see an individual as opposed to a stereotype drawn only from experience provided by the media. There should also be the opportunity to present people in unexpected roles such as women engineers, black teachers or disabled parents.

Choosing the visitor

It is usually not difficult to find a visitor. It could be someone from within the school, such as a member of ancillary staff, caretaker or teacher; or it could be someone from the community outside.

It can be difficult, though, to find someone who is confident, friendly and able to communicate with your children at their level. The main success of the visit will obviously depend on the visitor. It is not an easy experience, and people should be prepared for the unexpected. Children's questions can be direct, thought-provoking, provocative, threatening and even rude.

Preparing for the visit

Involve both children and visitor in any preparation beforehand. The children could:
• write a letter of invitation;
• prepare questions;
• learn to greet the visitor in any appropriate language;
• design and display a welcome sign;
• prepare a display of any items sent in beforehand by the visitor;
• make name signs for themselves in English and any other appropriate language;
• learn a special song;
• send the visitor a questionnaire.
The visitor could:
• send in some relevant special items,
whether cultural, religious, occupational or personal, such as photographs of home and family;
• send an outline autobiography around which the children could prepare questions
• reply to an invitation both in English and any other appropriate script;
• send in one or two 'mystery items' for children to research;
• answer a questionnaire.

The visit

During the visit there could be a number of activities rather than a straightforward question and answer session. The visitor could tell stories, sing songs, play a game, cook etc.

After the visit

Obviously after the visit there will be thank-you letters. It might also be appropriate to send a photograph of the occasion and maybe recall the visit at a later date by sending a card to celebrate an appropriate occasion, such as Eid, Diwali, Christmas etc.

Mathematics

'Because of the ways in which mathematics can be used as a means of communication it can play an important role in the learning process in curricular areas which may seem to be far removed from mathematics' (*Cockcroft Report*, Paragraph 485).

Mathematics, even more than science, is perceived as being culture-free, neutral and apolitical. Mathematics is undoubtedly a subject with high status. Children will spend a large percentage of their school life between the ages of five and sixteen in the pursuit of mathematical skills. If the argument that multicultural perspectives should permeate the curriculum is valid, then mathematics should have an important part to play.

Developments in recent years have suggested that teachers should consider the following strategies when planning their mathematics curriculum:
• Exploiting specific areas of the mathematical curriculum (some examples of possible areas for consideration follow);
• Examining the books and resources used in the mathematics curriculum;
• Making use of the opportunities within cross-curricular topics and themes.

History of mathematics

Mathematics is often considered to be somehow distinct and separate from the rest of the curriculum and consequently little attention has been paid to the history and development of mathematical systems and thought. Children should be allowed the opportunity to gain a wider view of the mathematical world and its

development over the centuries. This view should acknowledge the immense contribution made by Arabs, Indians and Chinese to the mathematical systems which are familiar to us. This is supported in the NCC consultative document *Mathematics for Ages 5-16*: 'it is right to make clear to children that mathematics is a product of a diversity of cultures.... Some attention to the history of mathematics could show the contribution to the development of mathematical thinking of non-European cultures; for example, it would be right to point out that the number system is of Hindu and Arabic origin.

Counting and calculating

This is a simple but useful activity which enables the teacher to emphasise the method shared by all cultures for simple computation. Even very young children enjoy learning to count to five or ten in a variety of languages. It is also interesting to point out the similarity in the names of numbers in many languages. For example, the word for three often begins with a 't', and the word for nine with a 'n'. The

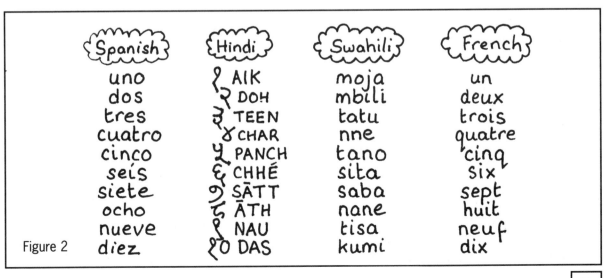

Figure 2

Spanish	Hindi	Swahili	French
uno	AIK	moja	un
dos	DOH	mbili	deux
tres	TEEN	tatu	trois
cuatro	CHAR	nne	quatre
cinco	PANCH	tano	cinq
seis	CHHÉ	sita	six
siete	SĀTT	saba	sept
ocho	ĀTH	nane	huit
nueve	NAU	tisa	neuf
diez	DAS	kumi	dix

following activity was used successfully with children between seven and twelve.

The children were given a basic information sheet as in Figure 2 on page 51.Groups or pairs of children were then assigned one of the languages and asked to learn to count from one to ten. This was then performed for the rest of the class.

Related activities could include the following.

- Simple calculations such as additions and subtractions using the names of numbers in the different languages, for example, 'six et sept = ?'.
- If rooms are numbered these can be 'translated' into other languages to form the basis of a 'language' or 'number' trail around the school;
- Older children could produce a counting frieze for younger children using different languages;
- Various counting games and songs could be adapted for other languages eg 'Ten green bottles'.

Games

There are many variations of chess, dominoes, and noughts and crosses in different cultures. These offer opportunities to explain rules and mathematical principles in an entertaining way.

Geometric patterns

Developing an awareness of spatial relations is an essential part of mathematical education. This can be explored by the use of rangoli patterns. Hindu and Sikh families design rangoli patterns to decorate their houses on special occasions, particularly during Diwali. The patterns could be used to explore pattern and symmetry through geometric forms.

In a similar way there are elaborate geometric patterns to be found in Islamic decorative art. These could be developed into activities on tessellation and symmetry.

Examining books and resources

It might be possible to argue that simple computation is culturally neutral, but that argument certainly cannot be extended to the books and materials which are used in the mathematics lesson.

There are many points to consider when thinking about resources. These could include:

- How much stereotyping of roles is there in the material? Are children from ethnic minorities always seen in passive roles?
- Do the text illustrations reflect the wide variety of lifestyles in modern society or is this variety largely ignored?
- Are mathematical developments seen as being solely a product of Europe?
- When children from ethnic minorities are included in examples and illustrations are they only there for show?

Further exploration of bias and insensitivity in primary mathematics material can be found in the excellent ILEA publication *Everyone Counts* (1985). This contains a wealth of ideas and suggestions, and shows that mathematics material can be biased and insensitive. Examples of insensitivity include:

- presenting a narrow range of lifestyles;
- ignoring or dismissing groups of people;
- perpetuating stereotypes;
- using offensive visual images.

The book also offers criteria for assessing mathematics materials and strategies for raising children's awareness of bias and insensitivity.

Making use of cross-curricular topics

Most mathematics course books do not respond to the issues posed by a multicultural society. It might be possible to find the use of ethnic minority names within examples and tasks, but this is usually as far as it goes.

It should follow, however, that in a genuinely cross-curricular topic which has taken account of multicultural perspectives there should be opportunities to reflect and support those perspectives within the context of mathematics. Many of those opportunities will arise within mathematics Attainment Targets 12, 13 and 14 in the National Curriculum. These are concerned with handling data. Programmes of Study between Levels 1 and 4, state for example, that pupils should be able to:

• Design a data collection sheet, record data leading to a frequency table;

• Construct and interpret frequency tables and block graphs;

• Use diagrams to represent the result of classification using two different criteria;

• Extract information from tables and lists;

• Enter and access information in a simple database;

• Construct and interpret bar charts and graphs (pictograms) where the symbol represents a group of units;

• Specify an issue for which data are needed.

A theme which has been developed with a strong intercultural perspective will, one hopes, include consideration of various relevant data, which could be interpreted in the ways outlined above. A topic on language and communication could include:

• A class, school, or neighbourhood survey on language variety;

- A study of the languages spoken in Britain;
- A study of world languages;
- An examination of the number of bilingual pupils in the school or town.

A topic on the media could include:
- An analysis of the frequency with which photographs showing people of various races appear in newspapers and magazines.

A topic on food could include:
- A survey of personal tastes, emphasising the right of people to be valued regardless of their differences.
- A survey on food preferences to show the cosmopolitan nature of British food.

Resources

The Story of Mathematics, Alistair Ross (A & C Black). This is a useful book for top juniors which describes how people began counting and measuring to help them solve everyday problems.
Count on Your Fingers African Style, C Zaslavsky (Crowell). This book describes the traditional finger counting methods of several different African peoples.
Tic Tac Toe, C Zaslavsky (Crowell). An interesting collection of various three-in-a-row games with information about the people who invented them, the rules and where they were played.

Science

While English may be readily accepted as fertile ground for encouraging multicultural development, it is certainly more difficult to persuade teachers of the role of science in this respect. According to some people, science is culture free, and it is a simple fact that most scientists are white and male and there's no way of getting round that!

Over the last few years, however, it has been strongly argued that science education in our multicultural society must include consideration of several factors.

The heritage of all

Science must be accepted as more than the preserve of Western European and North American cultures; it is the inheritance of all people. Since time began people have observed, measured, enquired, hypothesised, predicted, tested, evaluated and generalised. Societies have developed differently, so the content of science has differed from place to place.

The history of science

The historical context of science has been much neglected over the last few years. What information there has been has usually been presented as an aside and has almost always referred to the most important scientists, inventors and discoverers since the rise of modern science in the sixteenth century. Most children's knowledge of science is based almost exclusively on European or North American advances. Does it then follow that science is viewed as the natural possession of those regions alone?

The history of science is important. A full account would consider the achievements of most civilizations on earth, from Mesopotamia, Egypt and North Africa, Greece, China, the Roman Empire, Mayans and Aztecs, Central America, the Indian subcontinent, West Africa, Islamic civilizations in the East and Mediterranean through to the recent contributions in Europe, North America and the Soviet Union.

Considering resources

It is inevitable that the books and other resources which we offer to children present certain visual images along with their factual content. The resources used in science lessons are no different. On a simple level if we asked children to draw a scientist we would almost certainly receive the white-coated, slightly dotty male Anglo-Saxon professor. Science books still perpetuate these stereotypes, and we should perhaps be asking ourselves questions such as:
• Are all the accounts of scientific discovery and achievement taken from European or North American examples?
• Do the illustrations, whether cartoons, photographs or pictures, show only white faces?
• Are the references to the Third World negative (disease, poverty and starvation), without consideration of the wider reasons?
• Is it implied that only West Europeans and North Americans are scientifically and technologically advanced?
• What value judgements are conveyed by the use of words like 'simple' or 'primitive'?

How far does the National Curriculum support science teaching for a multicultural society? Before referring to these specific science documents it is important to refer again to the statements in the *Policy into Practice* document and paragraph 3.8 which states:
'The whole curriculum for all pupils will certainly need to include at appropriate (and in some cases all) stages ... coverage across the curriculum of gender and multicultural issues'. Science cannot be excluded from this.

The consultative document *Science for Ages 5-16* (August 1988) included a section on science and cultural diversity. The key points included:
7.12 Science education must take account of the ethnic and cultural diversity that the school population and society at large offers.... We recognise that interpretation of the nature of science may vary from culture to culture.
7.15 Science has a strong effect on a pupil's performance and this applies particularly to ethnic minority pupils. It is important that the pupils' own experiences should be used as a basis for learning.
7.16 More generally the science curriculum must provide opportunities to help all pupils recognize that no one culture has a monopoly of scientific achievement.... It is important therefore that science books and other learning material should include examples of people from other ethnic minority groups working alongside others and achieving success in scientific work.

There is still, however, a wide gulf between accepting the validity of these statements and translating them into classroom practice. Much will depend on the awareness of individual teachers.

Within the attainment targets laid down for science in the National Curriculum there are specific, well-defined areas in which it is clearly possible to make opportunities to relate ideas to a broad multicultural perspective. These include, for example, Attainment Target 2 'The Variety of Life' which states that for Key Stages 1-3 pupils at Level 1 should know that there is a wide variety of living things which includes human beings, and at Level 3 should be able to recognise similarities and differences between living things.

Attainment Target 4 'Genetics and

Evolution' states that for Key Stages 1-3 pupils at Level 1 should know that human beings vary from one individual to the next. There are obvious opportunities to foster positive discussion and investigation into skin colour, facial characteristics, hair and so on.

Attainment Target 17 'The Nature of Science' states that for key stages 1-3 pupils at Level 4 should be able to give an account of some scientific advance, for example, in the context of medicine, agriculture, industry or engineering, describing the new ideas and investigation or invention and the life and times of the principal scientist involved.

Here is the perfect chance to introduce and research into scientists who are not from the traditional white male model, such as the black Americans Charles L Drew who was a pioneer in the development of blood banks; Elijah McCoy, an engineer whose work on lubrication transformed railway systems worldwide; Percy L Julian who discovered a method to synthesise cortisone; and Jane C Wright, a leading specialist in cancer research.

It is clear then there are areas of science which would be incomplete without consideration of multicultural issues. But it often depends on the teacher's own sensitivity and awareness to ensure that the resources used in all aspects of the National Curriculum reflect the nature of Britain's multicultural society and that the images in those resources are positive, non-eurocentric and non-stereotypical.

It is only fair to acknowledge that many mainstream publishers are making great efforts in this direction. For example, the teacher who is using the cross-curricular theme of 'Ourselves' to meet various subject attainment targets might well use Franklin Watts' *Look at* series which includes *Eyes, Faces, Feet, Hair, Hands* and *Teeth*. The photographs are excellent, and show people from a variety of ethnic backgrounds. In some teaching situations this consideration of resources might well be the main focus for multicultural development. It should not be dismissed as incidental.

Resources

Third World Science, available from the Centre for World Development Education. This is a series of project pamphlets produced by the School of Education, University College of North Wales. The titles are *Carrying Loads on Heads; Charcoal; Clay Pots; Dental Care; Distillation; Energy Converters; Fermentation; Housing; Iron Smelting; Methane Digestors; Natural Dyes; Plants and Medicine; Salt; Soap* and *Pupils' Project from Zambia*.

Each pack has information and science activities from the Third World. The series has useful ideas which could be adapted and developed for work with top junior or middle school children.

Dictionary of the History of Science, Bynum, Browne and Porter (Macmillan). This is an excellent reference book which covers the physical, biological and human sciences, mathematics, medicine and the sociology and philosophy of science. It includes special articles on Chinese, Hindu, Islamic and other scientific traditions.

Science and Civilization in China, J Needham (Cambridge University Press). This is the most comprehensive account of Chinese science. It shows how Chinese science and technology were far in advance of Europe in many developments. Shorter versions are available.

Chapter Four

Foundation subjects

The *Policy into Practice* document recognises that 'a description of the curriculum in terms of subjects is not, of course, the only way of analysing its scope' (3.7). This view is further supported in Chapter Four of the same document. 'The use of subjects to define the National Curriculum does not mean that teaching has to be organised and delivered within prescribed subject boundaries' (4.3).

However, although there may not be a legal requirement for schools to deliver the foundation subjects under prescribed headings, 'what is required within each subject area will be defined and may be amended through Statutory Instruments' (*Policy into Practice* 3.5).

What this means for teachers is that much of the delivery of the National Curriculum in the primary school will take place through topic work. Teachers will, however, be required to take account of, assess and report on the ten foundation subjects individually.

This chapter will look at the foundation subjects in turn and the possibilities within them for exploring multicultural perspectives. It is made clear in the *Policy into Practice* document (3.8) that a great deal of the learning related to identified key themes, including 'coverage across the curriculum of gender and multicultural issues,' can and should be covered in the context of the foundation subjects.

History

It is unlikely that history will appear as a separate subject on the timetable of primary schools. As children move up through the years, though, there will be an increasing amount of historical study within topic or theme work. What should one consider when teaching history, and what opportunities are afforded to contribute towards preparing pupils for life in a multicultural society?

Multicultural history has often been misunderstood. It has been seen as seeking to teach about the history of ethnic minority pupils: to substitute, in effect, one area of content for another. This is clearly not adequate. The role of history teaching in terms of multicultural education includes:

• Encouraging children to recognise that every society has or had its own set of values and traditions. Any topic or theme looking at other societies and civilizations will, of course, address these areas. The aim should be, however, for children to avoid drawing conclusions that somehow these were or are exotic, strange or simply inferior.

• Ensuring that children realise that the movement of peoples is a universal phenomenon which has occurred since the beginning of time. Britain itself is evidence of this. This will hopefully contribute towards dispelling the ever-popular myths of immigration.

• Developing an understanding of the nature and value of historical evidence. This is clearly an area of controversy, particularly when the word 'bias' is used. Teachers should nevertheless encourage children to realise that historical evidence can always be presented from a particular point of view.

• Drawing on the different personal and family experiences that all children bring to the classroom.

• Avoiding the creation of stereotypes through an over-simplification of events. Telling the story of Captain Cook and how he was killed by 'natives' in the Sandwich Islands carries a negative message and is likely to be the only information children receive about the people who lived there.

• Providing opportunities for children to develop an understanding and awareness of the various community groups which make up the population of Britain.

• Ensuring that information books and teaching materials meet any agreed school criteria. Are the events so simplified as to be misleading? Are there any photographs or illustrations which are crude, inappropriate or offensive? Are the materials simply out of date?

Let us go on to look at a number of popular primary school topics or themes with a strong historical content, suggesting ways in which multicultural concerns can be identified and expressed.

Slavery

Slavery might be explored as a separate theme or as part of work on Britain's rise as a trading power. Teachers certainly approach this theme from the best possible motives. After all, it presents an excellent opportunity to bring man's inhumanity to man into sharp focus. What often happens, though, is that while the misery and plight of slaves is clearly highlighted there is often a disproportionate amount of consideration given to the abolitionists and their success.

Any investigation into the slave trade and slavery should include consideration of various factors.

African history

The enforced removal of people from their homes and communities must be placed in its historical context. Children's perceptions and images of Africa are, at the very least, inadequate and tend to be based on cartoons, comics and television. There should be the opportunity to present some evidence of the rich history of Africa. Slaves were not seized from the jungle. They were removed from long-established societies. The states of Ghana, Mali, Songhai and Benin were founded over 1,000 years ago. Their achievements were often envied by European visitors. In the sixteenth century Timbuktu was described as a city of learning and letters, with magistrates, doctors and men of religion.

Over-emphasis on misery

Clearly slaves were the victims of inhumanity, ill-treatment and cruelty. Teachers should, however, be aware that too much attention to the details of the voyages and plantation life with their attendant punishments and cruelties can perhaps convey the impression of the passive, willing victim. It is easy to become almost blasé about a constant catalogue of abuse.

Slave resistance

The role of the abolitionists is obviously of great significance, although it is not the only reason why slavery ended in Britain and its colonies. Few teachers include any discussion of the slave resistance which played a key role. Under the leadership of Nanny and her brother Cudjoe in the seventeenth century the Maroons developed an effective strategy of guerrilla warfare against the British in Jamaica.

There was also Maroon resistance in Dominica, St Vincent, St Lucia, Hispaniola and Panama. A totally successful rebellion of slaves was effected in Haiti under the leadership of Toussaint L'Ouverture.

Children should be aware that slavery is an unnatural condition and that people do not accept it willingly.

The legacy of slavery

One of the key aspects of history teaching must be the development of an awareness in children of how the present is rooted in the past. It is generally accepted that the vicious propaganda put forward to justify slavery as an acceptable state for black people has played an important part in shaping the attitude of white people towards black.

Slavery today

Children often suppose that slavery ended with its abolition in Britain in 1830. This is unfortunately not true. As defined by the United Nations in 1956 there are probably more slaves now than there were in Wilberforce's time. Modern forms of slavery include debt-bondage, child labour and slavery-like practices involving women. It is a fact that in 1985 more than 75 million children aged between eight and fifteen, most of them in the Third World were employed in some kind of work (International Labour Organization). In Thailand thousands of 13-year-old girls work 12 hours a day, six days a week making clothes for sale in well-known shops in the West.

Resources

The Atlantic Slave Trade (Avon County Council). This pack is a response to the County of Avon document *Guidelines for the Implementation of Policy Statement on Multicultural Education*. It uses a wealth of original source material, designed to support a wide range of learning styles, and it is intended as a contribution to the continuing debate on what makes good anti-racist history.

The pack consists of seven pupil booklets: *Parliamentary Enquiry - Role*

Play; Why was there an Atlantic Slave Trade? The Impact on Bristol; The Impact on Africa; The Impact on the Caribbean; Abolition Explained? and Changing Attitudes. Also supplied is a Teachers' Guide which provides detailed back-up to the pack and useful documents for discussion at department meetings.

Most of the activities have been tried out in Avon schools. The pack is available from Resources for Learning Development Unit, Bishop Road, Bishopston, Bristol BS7 8LS.

A Plantation Slave, Robin May (Wayland). Part of the How They Lived series, this book describes the life of a plantation slave in the American South.

Myths of Slavery (CAFOD). This is a useful set of six A3 posters which explode the following myths:

Myth 1: Slavery was abolished 150 years ago by William Wilberforce;

Myth 2: Child labour was abolished more than 100 years by Lord Shaftesbury;

Myth 3: Women have as much freedom as men;

Myth 4: All human beings are born free;

Myth 5: Apartheid enables people of different races to develop side by side in one country;

Myth 6: Tribal people are free to pursue their traditional way of life.

Ancient Africa, F Chijioke (Longman). This contains accounts of ancient kingdoms and their achievements.

The Story of Africa, B Davidson (Mitchell Beazley). This is an excellent resource for teachers.

A Visual History of W Africa, T Lucan (Evans)

The Caribbean People: Books 1 -3, L Honeychurch (Nelson Caribbean).

The African Experience Gladys Buck and Josephine Buck Jones (Millikien Publishing Co [USA]). This is a set of excellent

duplicating masters on African civilizations and societies, available from Gemini Teaching Aids.

Native Americans

The American West or Red Indians is another much-pursued topic in primary schools. It offers excitement, adventure and colour, but it is also an account of culture clash and dispossession. There are a number of key issues which teachers should consider in handling this theme.

Stereotypes

Simply asking children to write down all the words they associate with 'Red Indian' can be an effective starting point. A variation would be to ask children to draw a 'Red Indian'. There will no doubt be a common list of words including scalping, head-dress, savage, buffalo. You only have to close your eyes to imagine what the drawing will be like. It is certain that none of the children will have drawn anybody in contemporary clothes with any of the accoutrements of modern life.

From this 'brainstorm' there should be a scope for much useful discussion. Where do we get our images from? Are all Indians like this? Why do we only think of Indians as an historical anachronism? Most of the images will have come from countless repeated films. There should be some discussion of the power of television and its responsibilities.

Red Indian or native American

Just as the Inuit of the Arctic regions are wrongly called Eskimos, so it is inappropriate to continue referring to the various tribes as 'Red Indians'. Of course it is important that children should know where this label came from, that Columbus thought he had arrived in Asia and that the people's skin colour was not the same as that of Europeans. It is not useful, however, to continue using an inaccurate label with all its attendant stereotyped images. Drawing attention to points like this might appear to be trivialising the issues and merely contriving a response in multicultural terms, but when we add up all the small contributions we can begin to see change on a wider scale.

Issues of dispossession

Any discussion of native Americans must include consideration of the way in which white settlers systematically occupied the traditional lands of the various tribes. The allocation of reservations can be explored and parallels drawn with South Africa and Australia.

Human rights and native Americans

Native Americans today are very much an anonymous minority, far from the forefront of American life. There should be useful opportunities for children to consider what it is like being an outsider. This could lead to a discussion of various minority groups close to home, and to the consideration of human rights on a world level.

With upper juniors, teachers could use some of the simulation games and activities outlined in Chapter Six and Seven, including 'Rafa Rafa', 'Insider, Outsider', 'Stereotypes' and 'We want to be your friends and live in peace'.

Resources

World Studies 8-13, Fisher and Hicks (Oliver and Boyd). This contains useful section on minorities, including Native American issues.

Minorities, D Hicks (Heinemann). The central theme of this book is 'the crucial role of majority/minority issues in the world today and the need for students to understand the nature of such issues'. There are sections on experimental learning, a full-length simulation game and a helpful resources section.

Human Rights - An Activity File, Pike and Selby (Mary Glasgow Publications). This consists of 28 student-centred activities with photocopiable worksheets. It is designed for students of all ages.

Do it Justice!, Development Education Centre, Birmingham. This book is a practical handbook of resources and strategies. Its introduction asserts 'In order to understand the world in which we live, it is important that we understand the concept of human rights and freedoms and the ways in which people secure their social, political, economic and cultural rights'.

Plains Indians of North America, Robin May (Wayland). This is part of the *Original People Series*.

Return of the Indian Spirit, Phyllis Johnson (Grosvenor). This is a contemporary story of a boy who reaches a new awareness of his culture through a visit to his great grandmother. Suitable for top juniors.

The World Wars

World War I and World War II are themes frequently explored at upper junior level. There is often a sharp focus on the impact of the war on the local area or community.

The overriding impression can be that during the two World Wars Britain was standing alone until the entry of the USA. What is often forgotten is the indispensable contribution of the Commonwealth.

Considering this contribution should provide an excellent opportunity to continue dispelling some of the myths about immigration. Children should begin to understand that Britain was viewed as the Mother Country and that all citizens of the Commonwealth were expected to respond to her call. In wartime this meant joining the war effort, and in peacetime it meant responding to the call for help in rebuilding Britain's shattered economy.

Children should also have the opportunity to examine the accuracy of historical evidence and discuss its possible messages and interpretations. It is a fact that thousands of Commonwealth troops fought in defence of the Mother Country, either in their own lands or across the world. This was despite often being treated as second-class citizens in their own countries.

Total numbers of British, Dominion, Indian and Colonial troops who fought in World War I:	
British Isles	5 704 416
India	1 440 437
Canada	628 964
Australia	412 953
South Africa	136 070
New Zealand	128 525
Other Colonies	134 837
TOTAL	8 586 202
War Office Statistics 1922.	

About a third of the soldiers who fought for Britain in the two World Wars were from the Commonwealth, and about one eighth of these were black.

This information, however, is not often represented in popular textbooks. It is almost impossible to find photographs of black soldiers. Children could be encouraged to look at the statistics and to carry out research among the books on the two World Wars to look for information, photographic and written, which reflects the Commonwealth contribution. This could lead to a discussion of the practice of selecting the evidence to fit one's message. The work could extend into looking at more contemporary issues, such as the portrayal of minority groups in newspapers and so on.

Resources

'Together' - The Forgotten Contribution of the Black Commonwealth on the Two World Wars, Erica Pounce (from *Multicultural Teaching* Volume III Number 3 Summer 1985).
Black Settlers in Britain 1555-1958, File and Power (Heinemann).

Voyages and journeys

Most primary school children at some time carry out work around the topic of voyages. For many this falls under the heading of 'Voyages of discovery'. The focus of this theme will inevitably be the voyages out of Europe to the Caribbean, the Americas, Africa and the Far East. Europe is perceived as the centre from which all human curiosity, initiative and enterprise radiates. Even the very title carries the heavily loaded message that somehow the rest of the world was lying dormant in readiness for the arrival of the Europeans.

Of course Britain is in Europe and our first hand experience is of Europe but this does not mean that our curriculum should be exclusively eurocentric. Teachers should consider content carefully, and also the attitudes which they convey to the children.

If a topic or theme called 'Voyages of discovery' simply makes reference to European voyages, what messages are conveyed to the children? By referring only to European voyages there is an implication that somehow the rest of the world is lagging behind. Would it not be preferable to think in global terms and to see exploration as a part of the natural curiosity of the whole human race?

A topic around this area could include discussion of how people behave when they meet other people or visit a different environment. The activities 'Rafa Rafa' and 'We want to be your friends and live in peace' (see Chapter Six) are excellent ways to give children direct experience of the difficulties involved in communicating with and understanding other cultures.

'Insider, Outsider' is another useful starting point. For this the teacher marks each child with a different coloured sticker on the forehead. There should be about four different groups of Insiders - red, yellow, green and blue, for example. The children cannot see their own distingushing mark. A few children, the Outsiders, have different stickers both from the Insiders and from the other Outsiders. The children then try to form groups communicating only by gestures. No talking is allowed. The activity throws up a lot of talk and discussion about what it's like to be an 'Insider' or 'Outsider', how could we have made it nicer etc.

One could also include examples of voyages from the whole world, and not just Europe. There are obvious difficulties here for the teacher in terms of resources. European historians recorded the voyages of Europeans, and these accounts form most of the material available from mainstream publishers. There is, however, some material (see Resources), and it should be possible to include reference to the voyages from South America to the Pacific islands as reconstructed by Thor Heyerdahl in Kon-Tiki; the voyages of Cheng He, a fifteenth century Chinese Moslem who reached

Zanzibar in ships three times as large as European vessels; and the travels of Ibn Battuta, an Arab explorer whose wanderings rival those of Marco Polo.

One might also examine the concept of eurocentricism. The Mercator map projection produced in the sixteenth century placed Europe firmly in the centre of the world. A quick glance at the globe shows this is to be patently untrue. The activities suggested in Chapter Six, based around the Peters map projection, could help to lead children to a better understanding of the difficulties of mapping and the hidden messages conveyed by the very maps we use.

It is also useful to consider the effects of these voyages on the people involved. How many topics on Christopher Columbus concentrate on the glamour and excitement, on his triumph over disappointment and setback? The effects on the Caribs and Arawaks of the Spanish seizure of the Caribbean were much less glamorous: within 20 years of Columbus' first arrival the population fell from 360,000 to less than 40,000. Virtually a whole race was systematically exterminated: it cannot be right for such a topic to ignore this. The implications of the European landings for the Aborigines must surely be more important in conceptual terms than the celebration of the 200th birthday of Australia. Looking at the history of countries and peoples before colonisation of Europeans can be a revealing exercise. As we have already said, 'discovery' is a dangerous word. The voyages from Europe outwards to the rest of the world were not journeys to uninhabited countries. On every occasion the Europeans encountered well-established civilizations whose achievements matched and often outdid their own. In South America, Africa, India, China and elsewhere there were great kingdoms and empires and marvellous achievements in science, literature and the arts. It is important that children are aware of this and are not led to think that somehow the rest of the world was Europe's birthright.

Resources

World Travellers and Explorers, Derek Merrill (Edward Arnold).

Irish history

Finally it would seem appropriate to make some mention of the handling of Eire and Northern Ireland in the classroom. Most children will be aware, more vividly at some times than at others, of the current situation in Northern Ireland. No doubt many will ask questions of their teachers as events are reported on television and in the newspapers. For the majority these images will undoubtedly be the evidence on which they begin to form impressions of and perhaps prejudice or antipathy towards Ireland and Irish people. The issues are complex and difficult to explore with primary age children. A useful resource to introduce junior children to a wide range of Irish materials is *Irish Cultural Studies: A Teaching Pack* by Tom Arkett available from Trentham Books. The pack comprises two teachers' guides and 14 booklets including information sheets, maps, pictures and puzzles. There are three main sections: Ireland Today, Ireland's Cultural Heritage and Irish Migration. They consist mainly of small booklets including Irish personal names and surnames, Irish recipes, Irish poems, music, song, dance, major episodes from Ireland's history and the experiences of some Irish immigrants in Britain.

Geography

Most geographical work in primary schools takes place within topic work or in some form of integrated studies. Bennetts (1985) identified a number of key objectives for teaching geography in the early years (5-8) and in the later years of primary school (8-11).

He argues that the curriculum for the early years should, among other objectives, help pupils to:

• Develop an awareness of cultural and ethnic diversity within our society whilst recognizing the similar activities, interests and aspirations of different people.

• Develop an awareness of seasonal changes of weather and of the effects which weather conditions have on the growth of plants, on the lives of animals and on their own and other people's activities.

• Begin to develop an interest in people and places beyond their immediate experience.

For pupils in the later primary years the curriculum should help them to:

• Study some aspects of life and conditions in a number of small areas in Britain and abroad which provide comparisons with their own locality. From such studies pupils should gain knowledge and understanding of some of the ways in which people have used, modified and cared for their surroundings and of the influence of environmental conditions, culture and technology on the activities and ways of life of the present inhabitants.

• Gain some appreciation of the importance of location in human affairs and some understanding of such concepts as distance, direction, special distribution and spatial links (especially the movement of people and goods between

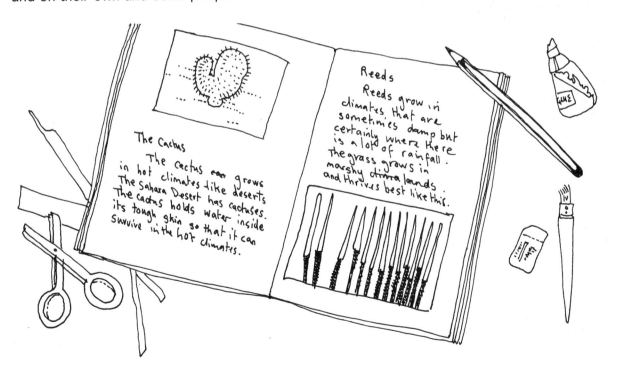

places).

• Develop an appreciation of the many different life styles in Britain and abroad which reflect a variety of cultures, and develop positive attitudes towards different communities and societies.

Geography for primary age children is mostly set within their own local environment and relates issues and explorations to their own experiences. In the later years of the primary school, however, there tends to be a move towards developing an awareness of places further afield.

Focus on a particular part of the world can be developed in a number of ways. Interest may have been sparked by a response to a news item. Many classes have developed projects on Ethiopia as a result of the famine and the work of organisations such as Band Aid. Others use major sporting events like the Olympic Games or the World Cup as a springboard. Some projects arise out of the teacher's own interest or the family experiences of some of the children.

It is likely that projects based on 'abroad' will include looking at similarities to and differences from the local environment, people and their way of life, the appeal of the place, the physical features and its links with other places. The highly recommended publication *Theme Work - Approaches for Teaching with a Global Perspective* (DES Birmingham) identifies the following 'challenges' which arise from teaching about a particular country or area, in this case, Tanzania.

• What do we really want the children to gain from looking at Tanzania?
• How far is knowledge about Tanzania important?
• What is the role of children's attitudes in this project?
• How do we counterbalance negative images of Tanzania?
• How far do we make links or connections between the children's experience and aspects of life in Tanzania?
• How do we introduce the children to new experiences without making them seem exotic or oversimplified?
• How do we teach with relatively few resources?
• How far do we look at the political context of Tanzania?
• How do we help children understand that they are only learning about a small part of the life in Tanzania?

In order to meet these challenges teachers should be giving consideration to three main factors; bias and stereotyping, teaching about minorities and resources.

Bias and stereotyping

Children will undoubtedly have their own mental maps of the world as well as ideas about what the people are like. Most of this information will have been acquired through the media, mainly television, and will be of varying quality and accuracy. Images built up through thoughtful documentaries and positive information programmes will have been countered by the plethora of outdated films and adventure series set in exotic locations. Any topic work based around another country must address these issues.

Teaching about minorities

Desert people, Arctic people, native Australians, native Americans and rainforest people are among the most popular minorities selected for detailed investigation. These studies offer opportunities to look at different lifestyles,

Prejudice

Will the study acknowledge the presence of prejudice and discrimination in majority/minority situations?

Origins

Will the study consider the origins of the minority situation, eg colonisation, migration, separatism?

Empathy

Will the study attempt to foster sensitivity and empathy for the minority experience? Will it attempt to combat prejudice in any way?

social structures, the effect of the environment and people's adaptation to it. In *World Studies 8-13*, Fisher and Hicks offer the following checklist of things to think about.

Motives

What are your reasons for choosing to teach about a particular minority group? Is it merely because they appear colourful or quaint?

The present

Will the study look at the present situation of the particular minority as well as its past and at the issues which confront its members today?

Status

Will the study show the social and economic status of the minority group and its disadvantaged position in society as regards the majority?

Culture

Will the study look at the minority group's culture and history in a positive way, including views of minority group members themselves?

Victims

Will the study make it clear that the minority group itself is not the problem, or will it blame the victims for their own oppression?

Response

Will the study show the breadth of minority response to discrimination, ranging from despair to direct action?

Self-esteem

What would be the likely effect of this study on the self-image and self-esteem of children from that, or other, minority groups?

Resources

An Arctic Child (Greenlight Publications). This active learning pack for eight to 13 year-olds examines our relationship with the Arctic and some of its peoples, such as the Inuit and the Sami. Topics include peoples of the Arctic, the Arctic ecosystem, seasons and temperatures, hunting and whaling, threats and pressures. The pack also includes an imaginative simulation game.

Tomorrow's Woods (Greenlight Publications). This is an active learning pack which aims to increase understanding and awareness of the importance of woodlands to life on this planet. It encourages children to 'think globally' and 'act locally'.

Life in the Desert (Green Deserts Publication, available from the Centre for World Development Education). This is a cross-curricular active learning pack about the desert environment, for eight to 13 year-olds. It presents a case study of Sudan which includes 26 activities exploring the issues of desertification, with posters and photographs.

Town-World Links (Development Education Project, Manchester). This is a pack of materials designed to help students undertake project work. Although written with 14 to 16 year-olds in mind it has been used successfully with top juniors. It encourages exploration of links between the local environment and the rest of the world, and contains a teacher's booklet, posters and student booklets on communities, the media, industry and work, aid and doing your project.

The Gwembe Valley Project in Zambia: Harvest Help, available from the Centre for World Development Education. This is suitable for children of ten upwards. It is a practical case study which contains eight study units, illustrated posters, 20 colour slides, maps and teachers' notes. All material may be copied for classroom use.

Project Focus Packs, (Christian Aid). Each pack contains background information, visual material, photographs and case studies of development projects. Titles include *Focus on Brazil, Focus on Central America, Focus on the Sahel, Focus on South Africa, Focus on Bangladesh*.

Development in Kenya, (Centre for World Development Education). These are five teaching packs containing 20 slides, with notes and worksheets compiled by teachers on the South West Development Project's Study Visit to Kenya. Their aim is to help teachers compare the different issues in Kenya and their own locality.

People Before Places - Development Education as an Approach to Geography, (Development Education Centre [Birmingham]). The ideas in this teacher's book have been developed by a group of geography teachers interested in introducing a critical approach to teaching about other parts of the world. Ideas are included for discussing population, aid, hunger and tourism, and for introducing development in a local context.

Theme Work - Approaches for Teaching with a Global Perspective, (Development Education Centre [Birmingham]). The ideas set out here have been developed by a group of primary teachers. The book includes a section of basic approaches for group work and includes guidelines for planning themes with a global dimension. Four themes are given to illustrate different approaches: *Images, Change, Transport* and *Tanzania*.

Geography from 5-16; a View from the Inspectorate, T Bennetts (1985) in *Geography* 70.4.

Art

Visual art is one area of the primary curriculum in which it is natural to include a strong multicultural element. There are countless opportunities to draw upon a variety of art forms and traditions. It is important, however, for children to recognize and accept that many of these art forms, whilst originating in other parts of the world, now form part of the cultural heritage of Britain. They are part of the contribution all migrants make when moving to new homes. Mehndi (henna), for example, is used for painting hands and feet at festivals and celebrations in Pakistan and some parts of India. However, setting the practice solely in an Asian-subcontinent setting will doubtless reinforce the view that this is something foreign, and that the people who practice the art in Britain are by equation also 'foreign'. It is surely better to view it also in its British context.

Drawing examples from a variety of worldwide cultures should enrich children's experiences and enhance their awareness. The message should be that these art forms have developed as responses to social, religious, economic, geographical and historical factors. They are no less valuable or imaginative than western art.

Much art work will arise as a result of the stimulus offered through the other foundation subjects. Art *per se* could, however, play a strong role in initiating discussion on skin colour in the context of racism and prejudice. Poster art can also be used for work on images, stereotyping and hidden messages.

Resources

Cross-cultural Art Booklets, Iain Macleod-Brudenell (Nottingham Educational Supplies). There are four titles in this series *Papercuts*, *Masks*, *Design* and *Clay*. Each booklet draw on a rich variety of cultural traditions and offers both background information and practical ideas.

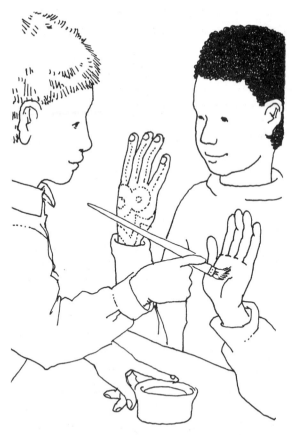

Traditional Designs from India, Mosaic and Tessellated Patterns, Japanese Design Motifs, Treasury of Chinese Design Motifs, Painting in Islam, Designs and Patterns from North African Carpets and Textiles, Arabic Art in Colour, African Designs from Traditional Sources and *Mola Designs* are available from Dover Publications. There are also Dover colouring books, which are not just time-fillers but contain useful information. Titles include *Celtic Design, Japanese Prints, Islamic Patterns, Maya Design, North American Indians, North West Coast Indians,* and *Plains Indians. Some Crafty Things to Do,* Karen Hale (Oxfam). This book includes information and ideas for various art activities including body decorating, batik, Indonesian shadow puppets and adire cloth (Nigerian tie and dye).
Alaro an activity pack based on traditional textile production in Nigeria (Oxfam). This pack is designed to introduce development issues into art activities. It focuses on a specific example of artistic expression from South West Nigeria. This pack offers basic principles of design for children to practise for themselves. *Exploring Asian Crafts in Britain* (Mantra Books). This series focuses on the craftsperson and discusses the history and origin of the arts. It contains simple instructions for projects work. Topics include *Puppets and Mask Makers, Mendhi, Rangoli* and *Pattern Designers.*

Music

Not all teachers are music specialists and even those who are cannot be expected to be familiar with all types of music. Nevertheless it is important that children enjoy a varied musical experience which is not confined to narrow limits.

The various communities which have settled in Britain over the centuries have brought with them a rich variety of musical traditions. Children should be encouraged to accept different musical styles and musical instruments as valid cultural expressions. They should react to new musical experiences without resorting to instant judgements and stereotyped responses.

The teacher's role here is the key. If she presents 'different' music as exotic and strange then the children will react accordingly. The attitude is clearly as important as the content.

Children's musical experience can be enriched to include a strong multicultural dimension in a number of ways.

Musical instruments

Many schools ensure that they have musical instruments from a variety of cultural traditions. All instruments are of value and they each have their own roles to play in music-making. The instruments should not be seen as being just for special occasions. It is heartening to note that although steel bands have often been dismissed as tokenistic they have fast become part of the accepted music tradition in many British schools. The National Steel Band Festival is held annually at the University of Warwick and attracts entrants of high quality from all areas.

Ensuring that children see and use musical instruments to make music and not just as artefacts with curiosity value should promote a positive attitude to the more unfamiliar instruments.

Using songs

There are many collections of songs available which can be used to introduce children to the music of different cultures. Songs can also be used to raise specific issues associated with multicultural education.

Performers

There are many professional performers who visit schools. Their presence as 'experts' can encourage children to see different musical styles in a more positive light.

Resources

Galt Educational offer a variety of musical instruments including shekeres (a natural dried gourd shell strung with a loose net of beads or seeds), bamboo rasps, an Ashanti pod bell with beater, tabla (Asian drums), monkey drums, cane rattles and gato drums.

E J Arnold has sections in its catalogue devoted to *Sounds of Africa, Sounds of Asia* and *Latin Percussion*. A comprehensive range of instruments is available.

Unity Learning Foundation supply some excellent posters and charts including *Music Around the World 1* (Australia, Bali, Brazil, China, Kenya, Peru, Scotland, Sri Lanka); *Music Around the World 2* (Guatemala, India, Japan, Nigeria, Papua New Guinea, Switzerland, United States, Wales); *Music Around the World 3* (Austria, Ghana, Hungary, Ireland, Pakistan, Sarawak, United Arab Emirates, West Indies). Each set contains eight charts which illustrate the wide range of traditional music-making around the world. *Instruments Around the World*, Andy Jackson (Longman). Each section of this book deals with one instrument and the culture to which it belongs. It includes instructions for making the instruments from everyday materials and explains how to play pieces using them.

The Singing Sack compiled by Helen East (A & C Black). The 28 stories in this book each contain a simple song with which children can join in as the story unfolds. The stories are taken from a variety of cultures and countries including Scotland, Sierra Leone, Japan, Zimbabwe, Russia and North America.

Birds and Beasts, Sheena Roberts (A & C Black). This book contains songs, games and activities about the animal kingdom, drawing on a variety of cultural traditions.

Mango Spice, Gloria Cameron, Yvonne Conolly and Sonia Singham (A & C Black). This collection has 44 songs arranged in themes with background notes, games, stories, dances and recipes from the

Caribbean.

Sing for Your Life - 44 Songs to Change the World, Sandra Kerr (A & C Black). An excellent collection on a variety of themes which will arouse thought and discussion.

Festivals Jean Gilbert (Oxford University Press). This anthology, for which a cassette is available, includes a short introduction to each festival, with classroom activities including art, craft and music, information about recipes and festival food, songs and singing games, and other useful information. Festivals include Harvest, Sukkot, Hallowe'en, Diwali, Christmas, Chinese New Year, Carnival and Eid-Ul-Fitr.

Religious education

Religious education is already a statutory requirement for all pupils in county and voluntary schools (except for those in nursery classes or where parents request otherwise), and in county and controlled schools is to be taught according to the local agreed syllabus.

Religious education teaching has forged many strong multicultural links. For many teachers multicultural teaching is certainly identified with religious education teaching and it can be difficult for them to understand that the same perspectives are equally valid and necessary in other areas of the curriculum.

Religious education is probably the best area of the curriculum as regards resources. Many multicultural centres have developed excellent materials and the major publishers have been quick to respond to the demand for attractive well-produced books and teaching aids.

A considerable number of local education authorities now have an agreed syllabus for religious education which recognises that Britain is a multi-faith society. For example, Warwickshire LEA has formulated a set of guiding principles relevant to the local agreed syllabus for religious education. They are as follows:

1 Religious education is an essential part of the education of all young people.

2 Religious education attempts to develop children's understanding of religion. It is different to religious nurture which sets out to raise a child within a particular religious tradition.

3 Christianity will be studied as the major living faith in this country but other religions will be studied in depth to enhance children's understanding of a multi-faith society.

4 Religious education should not be overburdened with factual information. It should concentrate on religion as people try to live and practise it today. Ample time should be allowed for reflection, discussion and response by pupils.

5 Teachers should adopt the same professional approach as they apply in other areas of the curriculum. Commitment, or lack of commitment to a particular faith on the part of the teacher is not an obstacle to successful religious education. It requires of teachers a commitment to enable children to explore religious experience.

6 Religious education stands in its own right within the curriculum. It is not identical with multicultural education, although, of course, it is an important element in this area.

7 Religious education is concerned with the exploration of feelings and attitudes as well as with concepts, beliefs and rituals. The media of the expressive arts are therefore important as well as skills and techniques associated with the humanities and social sciences.

8 Religious education is to be seen as a continuous process. Much of the learning will be based on direct experience and the sensitive teacher will reinforce and extend this with the use of references and materials appropriate to the age and level of understanding of the children. Even the youngest children can be introduced to explicitly religious material if it is carefully chosen.

In general the requirements for religious education will be met within topic or theme work rather than as a separate subject area. There will, however, be occasions on which RE will be the main focus.

Caring and sharing

A topic on caring and sharing, might develop an explicit RE element through consideration of raising money for charities, church collections, Zakat in Islam, the provision of meals in the Sikh langar and the Salvation Army, caring for the buildings and visiting the sick and elderly.

Implicit to this theme would be exploration of caring and sharing within groups, in school and in the family. Issues of the handicapped, the homeless, the old and infirm would certainly need to be raised.

Presents and gifts

In similar vein a topic on presents and gifts would contain explicit references to various practices in the major religions, and could include studies of Christmas, Eid or Hanukah. The implicit content would be to investigate the feelings and emotions generated by gift-giving and receiving, to consider why we give them, and to ask why the poor should have to receive charity.

Journeys and moving

As well as considering the children's own journeys or journeys made by famous people, this topic could look at pilgrimages within various religions including the Moslem Maj, Canterbury, Lourdes and Amritsar. Children could also look at their own lives as a journey and the various significant points along that journey, such as naming ceremonies, starting school, coming of age ceremonies and weddings.

Food

There are numerous opportunities within this topic to develop a strong multi-faith perspective. A discussion of what we eat and our food preferences could include an examination of religious dietary laws, such as kosher food, why Jews and Moslems don't eat pork, Catholics refusing meat on Fridays. Food is a basic human need; and discussion of this should make reference to the inequalities of food distribution throughout the world. Voluntary fasting for religious reasons can be compared with enforced hunger.

Buildings

The theme of buildings could be developed to encourage children to reflect on the significance of a place of worship for a religious community. This could encompass design and structure, furnishings, signs and symbols, and children's feelings when they visit a place of worship.

Obviously a visit to a place of worship

outside the immediate faith experience of the children needs to be handled with sensitivity. Parents must be clearly informed that these are purely educational visits and children will not be participating in any specific religious activities.

Clothes

It is likely that any topic on clothes will consider the clothes worn for special occasions, and those which have religious significance. This should provide opportunities to look, for example, at different wedding customs as well as special clothing worn by adherents and leaders of the major religions.

Rules

As well as investigating such things as safety rules, game rules and school rules, there could be some discussion of, for example, Moslem rules about prayers and the preparation for prayer, the ten commandments of the Jews and Christians, Hindu rules on food and so on.

Resources

The following packs offer excellent suggestions and ideas which focus on a particular festival but which contain a wealth of background information.
Approaches to Eid-Ul-Fitr, Multicultural Education Centre, Bristol.
Celebrating Festivals: Eid-Ul-Fitr, Multicultural Education and Language Service, Oldham.
Eid-Ul-Fitr, Minority Ethnic Group Support Service, Blackburn.
Approaches to Diwali, Multicultural Education Centre, Bristol.
Celebrating Festivals: Hindu Diwali, Multicultural Education and Language Service, Oldham.
Diwali, Minority Ethnic Group Support Service, Blackburn.
Baisakhi and the Punjab, Multicultural Education Centre, Bristol.

Physical education

Traditional sports and games will undoubtedly form the central part of any physical education programme. However, there is much to be gained by introducing children to sports and games which are popular both in different communities within Britain and in other countries.

Sports and games are common to all cultures. Many games have their origins in one culture but have been amended as they travel across the globe. Enabling children to learn about and share in the recreational activities of other people is perhaps another small step in encouraging respect and co-operation.

Resources

World Sports and Games Pack, Moray House College of Education. This pack contains ideas and suggestions to introduce multicultural, co-operative and Commonwealth perspectives into the physical education curriculum. It includes sections on the origins of games, making your own games, games for disability, a games database and world links.
Games of the World, Unicef. This book describes more than 100 games and their variations. There are photographs, paintings and diagrams, as well as details of the historical background.

Chapter Five

This chapter will look beyond subject-based or cross-curricular topics to other aspects equally important to an education which takes account of the multicultural nature of British society.

Considering resources

It goes without saying that all the resources used by a school, whether they are books, packs, worksheets or audio-visual information, and whether they are in the classroom or library, have a central role in the shaping of children's attitudes.

One question to be addressed is whether or not schools should create separate display areas for multicultural books. It is often tempting to isolate those 'good' books which meet agreed criteria and to create a separate section labelled 'Multicultural'. The danger here, of course, is that the message given both to children and to other teachers is that these books are somehow different from other books. Multicultural issues become marginalised rather than being on the main agenda. The message should be that a library is inadequate if its books have been chosen without consideration of multicultural issues. Ideally all sections of the library should include positive, carefully chosen books. In reality building up to this will take a long time. It should be possible, however, to ensure that library sections, ielves or displays are organised in such a way as to give subtle or natural prominence to favoured resources.

How do we choose?

Developing sensitivity and critical awareness either in oneself or in others is not an easy task. Not everybody finds *Little Black Sambo* offensive and not everybody acknowledges the hidden messages in books which talk about aid and help given by the West to developing countries.

There are numerous checklists available which offer a plethora of criteria to be considered when looking at existing materials or choosing new ones. Using other people's checklists can be a sterile activity, though, and indeed checklists are often viewed with suspicion by classroom teachers. They can nevertheless be a useful stimulus to encourage one to think about the resources in a school. It is clearly preferable for staff to work together over a period of time within a school INSET programme or development plan. In considering criteria it will be important to take into account the date of publication. Is the information inaccurate or misleading because the book was printed a long time ago? It is also useful to consider what to do when the criteria have been applied and there are no books left as a result and no money to buy new ones.

Do we throw all the books away which the guidelines expose as unacceptable? Of course the answer must be no. It would be naive to suppose that this would remove all pernicious influences from children's experience. If you measure the influence of the external media, such as television, newspapers or advertising, against the impact of the school's resources there is simply no contest.

In practical terms there will be some books which are inappropriate for the library or classroom. This may be because they are racist or sexist or out of date. There should be little argument against their removal. It is more difficult to know what to do with those books which contain more subtle, hidden messages either through the language used or through the illustrations. It might be fairly easy to recognise that a book on India has not provided a proper balance in its images. It is not necessarily easy to suggest a more positive alternative. Furthermore, cost will be a major factor. It is more realistic to suggest a gradual replacement process. Provided that teachers are aware of the powerful messages contained in books, it should be possible to use those unsatisfactory books in a positive way to enhance children's awareness. Teaching children to become critics, to devise checklists themselves and to apply them to the book on offer is of more lasting use than book-burning.

Where can I get 'multicultural' resources?
A few years ago teachers would probably have been pointed in the direction of the various LEA multicultural centres as being a principal source of multicultural resources. Many of these still produce excellent publications, but it is encouraging to note that most of the mainstream publishers are now offering more and more titles which attempt to meet multicultural criteria. Much of the demand for this has been generated by librarians, multicultural centres and

Welcome [welcome in other languages]

PARENT EVENING

teachers themselves. Although some publishers still retain specific areas of their catalogue for 'multicultural' books, most simply include these titles within cross-curricular sections.

In addition, there are many educational charities which are useful sources of material. The advantage of using these is that they offer excellent teacher-tested material at a reasonable price.

Display

The scenario can be described simply. The first-time visitor to the school in a predominantly white area, perhaps a prospective parent, approaches the school door. Displayed on it is a welcome sign in English and a number of community languages. What would be the inner reaction? If the other languages are exclusively Asian, I suspect that most visitors would be dismissive, not particularly interested or maybe even worse than that. It would be interesting to listen to talk among parents the day after a sign of this nature had been put up. It would definitely raise issues!

Here, then, is a common dilemma. Many schools are happy enough to see multicultural perspectives as an integral part of the curriculum. It is more difficult, however, to persuade the wider audience of parents, governors, casual visitors and ancillary staff.

Posters, notices, signs, children's work, artefacts, photographs and any other items of visual display can, however, form part of a school's statement about its philosophy.

It is nothing new for schools to try to convey an atmosphere of welcome and reassurance to visitors. The visit of a parent, governor or member of the public is an opportunity to show the school's philosophy in action. The visual displays around a school always say more than a sterile statement in a school brochure. A school's commitment to multicultural education should be part of these displays.

Information notices and signs

Around any school there are a number of written representations of language. This might be names of teachers, notice boards and headings, signs on doors (library, secretary, toilets, headteacher) and so on.

In a multilingual, multi-ethnic school it is both appropriate and necessary to ensure that information and notices are displayed in the major languages used in the school. Even in a predominantly all-white school, the writing on display can give an opportunity to celebrate diversity, create interest and foster a positive attitude towards languages other than English.

The Language Hunt activity described in Chapter Six within the topic on Language could be a natural way of introducing multilingual notices to a school. Once the children have completed the activity the signs could be left permanently around the school. A quiz-style letter could be sent to parents explaining the children's work and its effect on the school's appearance.

Similarly welcome notices could be put up as a direct product of children's work on language. As well as children producing their own posters and notices there are a number of commercially produced examples which could be used. Display phonetic versions of the 'welcome' word so that visitors can actually try out their linguistic skills and leave some paper for visitors to add new words. Even an apparently monolingual school will have a wealth of untapped talent and experience.

The 'welcome' notices could be extended at different times of the year to include appropriate festivals celebrated in the school.

Resources

The A2 *Welcome Poster* has 'Welcome' printed in 16 languages in full colour, and is laminated. It is available from Minority Group Support Service, Coventry.

A set of six multilingual signs printed in black on stiff white plastic sheets (A4 size) is available for office, library, staff room, reception, meeting room and notices. Each sign is in Bengali, Gujurati, English, Italian, Punjabi and Urdu. The set is available from Multiracial Education Resources Centre, Bedford.

A pack containing the word 'welcome' in English, Urdu, Punjabi, Hindi, Gujurati, Bengali, Chinese, Vietnamese, Italian, Polish and Arabic can enable schools to create their own posters. It can be obtained from the Minority Ethnic Groups Support Service, Blackburn. Also available is a Christmas Greetings pack which contains a 'Merry Christmas' greeting in the above languages in a large size suitable for display. There is also the 'Merry Christmas' greeting in the same languages plus Welsh, Norwegian, French and Spanish in a size suitable for putting inside Christmas cards.

Photographs

Chapter Three included a number of ways in which photographs could be used to raise multicultural issues. Responses produced by the children together with the photographs themselves would make a marvellous display for the entrance hall or reception area. If we believe that schools should be offering a positive representation of society to children, then it follows that the same should be offered to adults who visit the school. These issues are best raised with children through active learning, and in the same way displays can be used not as static representations but rather as opportunities to raise awareness of the same issues among visitors.

In one photograph activity, children use stickers to indicate which of the pictures they particularly liked or found interesting or unusual. This could be displayed and

assembly should be an opportunity to highlight particular areas of involvement and concern. It could focus on something already done or be a starting point which teachers can extend and develop within their own classrooms. Assemblies are an important part of the educational provision of the school. They offer an opportunity to reflect on life and our relationships with others, to celebrate and to share experiences.

Under the terms of the 1944 Education Act each school is required to begin the day with a corporate act of worship. The position of religious education has been strengthened under the ERA but no doubt teachers and schools will continue to establish and develop their own philosophies and practices within the legal requirements.

explained. Stickers could be left out so that visitors could also have the chance to contribute.

Another activity involves children asking questions about a photograph, while other children try to offer answers. A photograph could be left with a question for visitors to answer. In a similar way themes or topics such as languages or migration could be explained and enhanced by having questionnaires or survey sheets for visitors to complete.

School assemblies

Assemblies should not be seen as the only platform for raising the concerns and issues of multicultural education. A 15 minute assembly on the theme of injustice or inequality is unlikely to have anything more than a short-term impact. The

Resources

The Tinderbox Assembly Book: Starting Points, Stories and Classroom Activities, Sylvia Barret (A & C Black).
Hand-in-Hand Assembly Book, Russell Profitt (Longman). This contains over 50 assembly stories including folk tales and accounts of modern figures.
Assemblies for Development, Centre for World Development Education. This is a collection of assemblies on issues of world development. There are 15 themes, each with a scripted assembly, plus useful suggestions for extension work. The themes are Spring, Harvest, Health, Death, Poverty, Trade, Aid, Food, Deserts, Water, Conservation, Women, Racism, Migration and Peace.

Oxfam's Audio Visual Resources Unit has a wide range of resources available for sale and loan to teachers. They include postcards, slide/tape presentations, slide sets, videos, exhibitions, artefacts and everyday objects from overseas. Details from AVRU, Oxfam, 274 Banbury Road, Oxford OX2 7DZ.

Common Ground is an illustrated songbook containing 12 songs with full accompaniment, from Christian Aid. Christian Aid also offers a wealth of other useful materials including postcards, videos and information sheets.

Sing for your Life - 44 Songs to Change the World, chosen by Sandra Kerr (A & C Black).

First Focus, Redvers Brandling (Bell & Hyman). A collection of stories for assembly.

The Minority Group Support Service, Coventry, produces a number of assembly packs which contain overhead transparencies, scripts and teacher notes. The subjects are Harriet Tubman (a black woman who devoted her life to fighting slavery); Ghandi; Mary Seacole (a black woman who nursed throughout the Crimean War but without the recognition given to Florence Nightingale); Sri Guru Nanak (the founder of Sikhism); Martin Luther King; and the world of Islam.

Performances

School performances, whether they are plays, concerts, or musicals, can be an opportunity to convey much about the atmosphere, ethos and philosophy of a school. They can also encourage consideration and awareness of issues associated with multicultural education.

It goes without saying that the audience is there to be entertained rather than preached at. There are nonetheless a number of levels at which the school can promote its commitment and sensitivity.

On one level it might just be a case of including a variety of cultural items which recognise the different strands within a community. On another level it might be a case of rejecting certain productions as not conveying appropriate messages. Blacking children's faces, for example, whilst often done in ignorance, can perpetuate a stereotyped image of black people.

On a more direct level there might be a deliberate strategy to choose a play or musical with a strong message rather than to choose only for the sake of entertainment.

The World Wide Fund for Nature publishes two such musicals which combine powerful lyrics, excellent music and a high entertainment factor.

Yanomamo, by Peter Rose and Ann Conlon, tells the story of the Yanomami (forest people), a tribe which has lived for thousands of years in harmony with the rainforest environment in the Amazon basin. But poverty, greed and population growth in the countries surrounding them bring new pressures to bear on the tribe's way of life. The musical has been performed by many schools in Britain and in other countries. The *Yanomamo* cassette and word booklet is published by Josef Weinberger. The music manuscript is available from WWF United Kingdom Education Distribution.

Also written by Peter Rose and Ann Conlon is *African Jigsaw*. This musical looks with humour, irony, pathos and great vitality at the problems which can arise in cities. It seems the lesson is that human needs must be dealt with in a fair and just manner if sustainable use of the earth's resources is to be achieved. However, the musical itself does not attempt to solve problems, it simply places the fragments of the puzzle before us. The *African Jigsaw* score, cassette and word booklet are available from WWF United Kingdom Education Distribution.

Racist incidents

Behaviour of a racist nature can take a variety of forms. Some of these obviously have a more direct effect on people's lives than others, for example:
• Racist abuse directed at pupils, teachers, visitors or ancillary staff;
• Physical assaults on ethnic minority pupils;
• Name-calling;
• Writing offensive comments or slogans;
• Defacing illustrations in books;
• Racist jokes;
• Refusal to work with children from ethnic minority groups.

It is never difficult to persuade people of the effect of a physical attack, but it is not always an easy task to convince some teachers that racist jokes or name-calling, for example, merit serious attention within the discipline of a school. A great deal of sensitive discussion needs to take place at staffroom level. Even so, it will be impossible to convince everyone. This is perhaps another argument in favour of an agreed school policy which even minority dissenters must respect.

Is racist name-calling any different from 'ordinary' name-calling? If it is no different, then it is simply one of those things that in the main children have to put up with. However, notwithstanding that all name-calling is clearly wrong, there is a major difference. Calling someone a Paki, Wog or Coon is to assert that somehow these groups and all the people in these groups have the same inherent negative qualities.

To be labelled a Paki or Coon is to [...] labelled as bad. On the other hand [...] an individual 'Four Eyes' or 'Fatty' is not to denigrate by implication a whole race of people. Racist jokes are another area which can produce an ambivalent response among teachers. What's wrong with Paki jokes? Are Irish jokes racist? After all, the Irish tell jokes about themselves or about Kerrymen. The answer is, of course, that unless you happen to be a member of the minority group, it is very difficult to pass an opinion on whether such jokes are offensive or not. It would be surprising to find any child of an Asian background who said that she found 'Paki' jokes amusing. The truth is that these jokes are almost inevitably negative and offensive. Telling a 'Paki' joke in a predominantly white school is reinforcing stereotypes. The children in those schools do not have real people around them who can dispel those stereotypes by their very presence.

What ways are there then for a school as a whole or a teacher individually to respond to these forms of behaviour? Should racist behaviour simply fall within the established disciplinary procedure or is it to be viewed as warranting specialised individual attention?

Most schools which have formulated policies have included a section on racist behaviour and have suggested ways in which their own institutions can deal with it.

A number have devised elaborate structures and procedures in which every racist incident is recorded and reported at various levels to year heads, headteachers, parents and governors. Sanctions have included suspension and a series of compulsory counselling sessions after school before any re-admission is permitted.

might be to give a platform to members who can have a negative influence on others. Sometimes it might be more appropriate to have a quiet word with the people concerned at the end of the day or session. To ignore racist remarks consistently is to condone them, and this conveys a definite message to children.

• There should be a framework within the school so that teachers do not feel that they are alone in responding to events. There is little point in having an agreed school response if it is only followed half-heartedly by some staff.

• Any victim of racist behaviour should be supported positively.

• Graffiti on walls, furniture and books should be removed immediately.

• The only badges or insignia to be worn should be those connected with the school.

• The teaching style of the school should lend itself to pupils working collaboratively in groups.

Professional development

At a time when the innumerable demands of the National Curriculum are uppermost in teachers' minds it is important that the issues of multicultural education do not get pushed to the side. Delivery of the National Curriculum means delivery of a curriculum which has taken account of the concerns of equal opportunities.

Many schools now have named co-ordinators for equal opportunities (race, gender and disability) or specifically for multicultural education. Very often this is an unrewarded post of responsibility which

School policies generally offer advice along the following lines:

• Children and parents must understand that the school and all its staff, teaching and non-teaching, will not accept any form of racist behaviour. They must understand that this behaviour is unequivocally wrong. As such, it will be dealt with within the disciplinary framework of the school. The school's commitment to a fair multicultural society should be declared in its handbook or brochure.

• Individual teachers should not ignore racist incidents. At the same time there should be caution against over-responding. Teachers will use their own professional judgement. There will be occasions when an incident needs to be discussed with a whole group. At other times to do this

has been taken on by someone who is personally committed. This role could include:
• Ensuring that any LEA or school policy is consulted during the formulation of a National Curriculum Development Plan;
• Ensuring that colleagues are aware of the multicultural perspectives and opportunities within the National Curriculum documents;
• Disseminating information about appropriate INSET courses and training opportunities;
• Making sure that multicultural perspectives are reflected in discussions about aspects of school life;
• Liaising with outside agencies such as the Schools Library Service, to ensure that appropriate resources are available;
• Taking responsibility for an area of the staffroom noticeboard under the heading Equal Opportunities News or Multicultural News (this could include details of courses, events, important religious festivals and dates, newspaper cuttings, television programmes, social events, extracts from National Curriculum documents);
• Encouraging the school to subscribe to some specialist multicultural publications or to those publications whose philosophy is broadly sympathetic;
• Ensuring that the school receives details and catalogues from centres and agencies which offer excellent teacher-tried materials such as the Development Education Centre, Oxfam or Save the Children.

Resources

Journals, magazines and newsletters worth subscribing to include *Letterbox Library*, which is the only bookclub to specialise in non-sexist and multicultural books for children. It offers good discounts on hardbacks and a range of inexpensive paperbacks. There is a free member's newsletter full of information, available from 5 Bradbury Street, London N16 8JN.

Multicultural Teaching aims to combat racism in school and community. This is a termly journal which is concerned with all aspects of teaching and learning in a multicultural society. It contains academic, theoretical and practice-based articles. There are also reviews of new books and a wealth of information about courses, conferences and events. Back copies are available from Trentham Books Ltd, 151 Etruria Road, Stoke-on-Trent, Staffs ST1 5NS.

Dragon's Teeth is an excellent magazine published by the National Committee on Racism in Children's Books, which monitors the content of multicultural and anti-racist education. There are reviews of new books as well as short stories and poems by new writers. Back copies are available from NCRCB, 5 Cornwall Crescent, The Basement Office, London W11 1PH.

Issues in Race and Education is a termly independent journal which offers articles, reviews and information. Each issue is based around a specific area of concern. These have included *Mother Tongue: Policies and Practice; Section 11 - Who Needs Special Funding?; Measurement Assessment: What is Meant?; Media Matters; Shelving Books; Issues for Girls in Race and Education;* and *Anti-Racist Education - a new ERA?.* Back copies are available from *Issues in Race and Education,* 75 Alkham Road, London N16 6XF.

Green Teachers is a journal which assumes that teachers want to help children develop their understanding and skills in co-operating with and caring for the earth and each other across boundaries of all kinds and growing as independent, self-reliant and confident individuals. Some items have included *Global Perspectives*, *Tropical Rainforests*, *Peace Studies* and *Human Rights*. Materials to be used directly with teaching groups are provided in each issue. Limited back copies are available from Green Teacher, Llys Awel, 22 Heol Pentrehedyn, Machynlleth, Powys SY20 8DN.

Global Education News is an excellent newsletter (about ten pages) published four times per year. It contains news, details of resources for the classroom, some practical teaching ideas, details of events, courses and conferences. It is available from Centre for Global Education, University of York, Heslington, York YO1 5DD.

Junior Education and *Child Education* are both monthly magazines with a strong commitment to multicultural education. This is evident in the accounts of good practice, the areas of concern identified, and the reviews of recent books and publications. Subscription details are available from Scholastic Publications Ltd, Westfield Road, Southam, Near Leamington Spa, Warwickshire CV33 0JH.

School policies

Over half of the local education authorities in England and Wales have issued policy statements on multicultural and anti-racist education. Some local authorities have required schools to formulate their own policies or provide a response to the LEA policy.

Reaching agreed school statements is never an easy process. This applies whether the area of concerned is a reading policy or an agreed maths programme. Arriving at a consensus on a school policy for multicultural education

can be even more fraught. Whilst there may be differences of opinion about which maths scheme to choose, at least every teacher accepts that mathematics will be there. For many teachers, however, the issue of multicultural education is not understood and is certainly not a priority. Although the LEA may require schools to come up with a policy statement, there are serious training implications regarding the ability of schools to raise these issues. It will no doubt be much easier to convince the majority of teachers in multi-ethnic schools of the value of raising these concerns and formulating a response than it will be to get the same response in predominantly white schools.

There are several important questions which should be addressed.

What do we want a policy for?

The process of drawing up a school policy should be an important contribution to professional development within the school. It provides opportunities for discussion of important and sensitive issues which often get pushed to one side in the everyday work of the classroom. A policy is also a public statement of the philosophy of the school to the whole community.

Do we need a separate policy on multicultural education?

The danger of having separate policies on multicultural education is that multicultural education will continue to be seen as something distinct and separate from mainstream education. Conversely it could be argued that raising this as a separate issue demonstrates how vital and fundamental a school considers this issue to be.

Many schools have long, detailed policy statements on multicultural education drawn up carefully over a period of time. Whether these ever reach a wider public is open to doubt. Other schools have chosen to include in their handbook or brochure a short and simple statement on multicultural education, set within the context of the overall philosophy of the school. Some schools have preferred to include multicultural education in a broader policy statement on equal opportunities encompassing race, gender and disability.

Clearly the aim should be for teachers to take account of multicultural perspectives within the discussion of any aspect of the school's life. The reality is that without the reminder of a separate policy the issues will often be ignored.

What should a policy include?

Most policies, whether compiled by the LEA or the individual school, have included statements on many of the following points. Some of these will have more relevance for multi-ethnic schools.
• Curriculum;
• Ethos and atmosphere;
• Racist language and behaviour;
• School environment;
• Community involvement;
• Bilingualism;
• Resources;
• Monitoring and assessment of bilingual pupils;
• The implications of a policy for all staff, teaching and non-teaching, and the governors;
• Practical suggestions to translate policy into practice;
• The need to monitor, review and evaluate the policy.

The last item on the above list, monitoring, reviewing and evaluation, is crucial to the continued success and effectiveness of any policy.

During the period of formulation and consultation, the policy and the issues will enjoy a high profile. There will hopefully be a sense of ownership among all teachers, and there is usually a strong impetus from those charged with framing the policy. What follows, however, will be an inevitable loss of momentum. The school will be moving on to look at some other identified key area.

For those schools with large numbers of bilingual pupils it will be much more difficult to ignore what has been included in a policy statement. Issues of racist language and behaviour, assessment of bilingual pupils, community involvement and so on will continue to be part of everyday concerns.

In schools which are predominantly white, it is often hard to translate the smooth one-liners of a policy statement into practice. While it might be possible to monitor the performance of bilingual pupils in multi-ethnic schools, it is not so easy to measure attitude change in the all-white school.

Another factor in the success of the policy will be changes among the staff. Does a document which was originally agreed on by the whole staff continue to represent a shared decision? Has it rather become an inherited piece of paper? It is important that any policy statement is discussed with new members of staff, and that a chance is provided for them to contribute.

It is clear, then, that unless there is a structure which allows regular review and evaluation, the policy document becomes nothing more than a historical record of a certain period in a school's life. Of course it is invaluable as a declaration of where

a school stands on this key issue, but it must be more than that.

As with many aspects of education, success will in reality often depend more upon committed individuals than upon a shared effort.

Despite the fact that there will be conflicts between differing philosophies, and problems when translating policy into practice or deciding on an effective method of evaluation, it remains true that the process of considering where the school stands on multicultural education is of unquestionable worth.

Finally, it is worth considering the position of school policies in relation to the National Curriculum. The DES has advised that all schools should prepare National Curriculum Development Plans which 'will look over the early years of implementation of the National Curriculum'. The Development Plan 'should also help headteachers in looking across the curriculum to ensure that it meets overall objectives as well as specific statutory requirements and that concentration on the latter does not crowd out adequate attention to other subjects and issues.' (DES *Policy into Practice* 9.12).

The next few years will undoubtedly place great demands on teachers' time, patience and energy. It is hard to envisage the establishment of a great many school-based working parties on multicultural education. It is perhaps more realistic to suggest that consideration of these concerns and their implications for the school will take place within the broader framework of the School Development Plan, which should of course take account of 'Coverage across the curriculum of gender and multicultural issues' (DES *Policy into Practice* 3.6).

Chapter Six

Topics and themes

This chapter offers suggestions for developing the multicultural perspective within topic or theme work. As we have noted, the National Curriculum does not seek to organise teaching within prescribed subject boundaries; the emphasis is on the continuance in primary schools of strong cross-curricular themes. It is through these themes that the majority of primary schools will find their multicultural work developing.

The first point to consider about the relationship of topic work and multicultural education is that we must accept the wider definition of multicultural education as outlined in Chapter Two. Development education, gender issues, disability issues and environmental concerns must all be seen as contributing to the ultimate aims of education for a multicultural society.

The resources used for a topic, such as books, posters and photographs, should reflect the ethnically diverse nature of British society. It is not always possible, of course, for every topic to make direct reference to every ethnic group within Britain. What is possible is to ensure that within every topic there is a chance to raise awareness of issues such as human rights, hunger and famine, equal opportunities and so on.

The choice of topic then is another important consideration. Certain topics have a naturally strong and clear intercultural dimension. If a teacher has chosen the theme of 'Moving' for a class of ten and eleven year-olds, it is not difficult to see the opportunity to explore such issues as migration, attitudes to newcomers and difficulties experienced by newcomers.

Similarly, the topic of language and communication will offer scope for discussion of community languages in Britain, attitudes towards different languages, similarities between languages and bilingualism.

Planning a cross-curricular theme might mean identifying key activities and ensuring every subject area is represented. What is most important is that all strands, including the multicultural perspective, come together as a balanced whole. Few of us have such heightened sense of awareness that we can immediately spot the multicultural dimension or potential. Once we accept that it is there and that it is essential, the task becomes easier.

Moving

The myths of immigration still abound bringing with them prejudice and racism in both adults and young children. Immigrant is synonymous with Afro-Caribbean and Asian. Few people realise that the majority of settlers in Britain come from Southern Europe or Ireland. Few people know that in almost every year since 1956 more people have left Britain than have arrived.

Children must understand the composition of British society. If the white girl living in rural Cumbria visits her cousin in Manchester she should be able to understand why there are Asian or Afro-Caribbean families living in the same street and recognise that these people have had the same experience of moving as her own family.

Moving is a common human experience shared by most of us. This can easily be forgotten, however, in the presence of emotive words like 'immigration' or 'gypsies' or 'refugees'.

In this section a number of activities, considerations and starting points are suggested which can form the basis of a topic or theme on moving. The aim would be to heighten children's awareness of a common experience. Within the theme one could make reference to:
• Personal and family experiences of moving;
• Common emotions such as joy, sadness or fears;
• Reasons for moving (personal, economic, political and religious);
• Positive contributions made by newcomers (language, religion, culture, food or dress);
• Negative experiences of newcomers;
• Attitudes towards newcomers;
• Global links and connections;
• Britain as a nation of newcomers (Celts, Saxons, Normans etc).

Possible activities

Rafa Rafa
Rafa Rafa is available from Christian Aid and is described as a cross-cultural simulation game. Don't be put off by this description! Rafa Rafa is an excellent thought-provoking activity. It can be used at any point within a theme. I have had most success using it as an immediate hard-hitting first session.

The game illustrates difficulties and problems we may encounter when meeting people who are different from us. It highlights our irrational tendency to disparage, fear, dislike and distrust anything said or done by another person or group which we don't understand or find unfamiliar.

For the activity the children are divided

into two groups, Alphans and Betans. Each group occupies a separate classroom and is taught the rules for a different way of living. The Alphans are fun-loving and superstitious; they have great respect for their elders and they enjoy touching. Betans are hard-working and business-like, and do not like to be close to each other. Once each group has learned the rules of its own culture, observers and visitors are exchanged between groups. Their role is to try to learn about the other culture by first observing and then interacting. Gradually a picture of the other society is built up and the game ends when everyone has had the chance to visit the other society.

The groups then come back together and report their findings and conclusions about each other. What emerges is the difficulty we have in understanding other cultures, and the little effort we make to do so. During the discussion period children can be asked questions on the lines of 'What was it like to be a visitor?', 'How do you treat visitors?' or 'How could you have made it easier for visitors?'.

Follow-up activities have included recording the rules of each culture, representing the experience in poster form, or designing welcome posters for each group and then the school foyer. Another possibility is for each child to write a response to a statement like 'Playing Rafa Rafa today has helped me understand...'. The statements were then collected, and the children arranged them in order of importance.

I can recommend Rafa Rafa thoroughly. No teacher will be disappointed either by the activities or by the potential follow-up. It has also been used to support many other themes such as languages and communication, voyages of exploration and encounter, and homes and families.

Word House game
The Word House game is an exciting one, which has appeared in various forms. This account is based on the version available in *World Studies 8-13* (see Resources).

The game demonstrates that our everyday language is made up of words and phrases from all over the world. Many cultures have made valuable contributions to our speech. Words have travelled

because people have moved and made contact with others. Children's attitudes to 'foreign' languages often leave much to be desired. Hopefully activities like this can become part of the 'dripping tap' process whereby negative responses become less frequent and pronounced.

Divide the class into pairs and give each a list of 20 words and information about a particular language. All the words are now common 'English words'. There are eight language families represented: Celtic, Indian, Dutch, French, Scandinavian,

Italian, Greek and Latin. Each family has its own colour. The children are also given a 'word house' in which there are 160 bricks (8x20 words). The object of the game is to get as many bricks on the house coloured in their correct colour. This is achieved by moving around the room, visiting the different families and finding out which words on the house belong where. The session easily takes a morning or an afternoon.

Follow-up activities could include finding out more about the language families, finding out why and when particular words came to be accepted into the English language, and writing stories or poems based around each pair's 20 words. A large version of the Word House forms an ~xcellent display for classroom, corridor ~~ ambitious project could be mological dictionary to House to even more Spanish, Arabic, Inuit,

Moving survey
A survey on moving is a tangible way of stressing the commonness of the experience. Ask the children to do some preliminary research by asking parents and other members of their families questions about how long they've lived in the town, where they've moved from, reasons for moving, languages in the family, attitudes to moving and so on. Photographs of previous houses, towns and countries could be brought in.

The actual completion of the survey can take place in the classroom in pairs. Once finished the results can be collated to provide class statistics. Information can then be represented in the form of bar charts, tick charts, pictograms and pie charts. In one class of 30 children in an all-white school, 29 children had experienced moving house, 16 had moved more than once, 15 had visited another country and there were 11 languages represented in their different families, including Welsh, Irish and Scottish Gaelic, Polish, Italian, Swedish and Ukranian. The evidence of Britain's multicultural society was clear even in this all-white classroom.

The survey could be further extended throughout the rest of the year-group or school.

Using maps

Using maps is a simple but effective way of demonstrating visually and immediately how much effect moving has had on all our lives and how our lives are inextricably linked with different parts of Britain, and more importantly with the rest of the world.

For most children countries like Chile or Pakistan or Algeria are no more than words. If you were to ask them to 'brainstorm' all their ideas or images of somewhere like Venezuela I'm sure you'd get no more than one or two words in response. Using the experiences of the children is a simple way of showing that these places are real; they are more than names, because Pauline's Uncle James works there or Gurdeep's cousin lives there.

An effective way to display the information is to use three maps; one world map, one map of the British Isles and one of the town, district or neighbourhood. Give each child three different coloured map pins and ask them to place them as follows:
• One pin on the world map to show a place where they have a relative or a friend, or a country that they have visited.
• One pin on the map of Britain to show a place where a relative lives.
• One pin on the local map to show where they have lived before, or where a relative lives.

Once this has been done children could produce information cards for each pin, showing, for example, that Sarah has an auntie in Saudi Arabia. Other follow-up activities could include listing towns or countries with which the class has connections, and research into the reasons for those connections.

Reasons for moving

One aim of the topic on moving must be to dispel some of the more unpleasant myths about immigration: that Asians and Afro-Caribbean people came to Britain to scrounge; that they were always unwanted and that they've made no positive contribution to British society.

One of the questions in the moving survey (Figure 1, page 98) asked 'Why did you and your family move?' and offered a few possible reasons:
• Family reasons;
• Employment;
• Better housing;
• Forced to move from another country.

This question is an obvious starting point for raising questions such as the reasons for immigration and settlement and how it affects the local community, Britain, and the world. A wider list of reasons for moving might include being nearer to work, the cost of housing, marriage, religious persecution and escape from a war zone.

The different groups that have arrived in Britian over the last 2,000 years have had many different reasons for their arrival. It is not too difficult to research these reasons and to produce a set of cards similar to the ones in Figure 2 on page 99. Some of the cards can be used to reflect the local experience of particular communities.

Children can then work in pairs or groups

with the set of cards illustrating migration to Britain. Sharing the cards they can read them to each other and record on a matrix the reason for each group's migration.

Further work could include researching particular groups.

Using stories

Some teachers prefer to base their topic work around a book they are reading with the class. There are a number of stories which can be of use for themes based around the experience of moving. These include:

Journey of 1000 Miles, Ian Strachan (Methuen). (10-12 year-olds). This is an exciting, dramatic and moving story about the Vietnamese boat people. The book tells the story of Lee and his family who escape from Vietnam in an old leaky fishing boat crammed together with 40 other people. It is a story of hardship, danger, bravery and survival. It should form the basis for some excellent,

---

<u>Moving and Settling Survey</u>

1. What is your name?

2. Where do you live?

3. Have you moved to a different home during your lifetime? Yes / No

4. If you have moved, where did you live before?
   a. somewhere else in Britain? b. in another country?

5. What is the name of the village/town and country where you lived before?

6. How many times have you moved house?
   a. never   b. once   c. twice   d. several times

8. Why did you move?
   a. family reasons b. employment c. better house
   d. forced to move from another country.

Figure 1

thoughtful work on the difficulties experienced by refugees and the responsibilities we all have.

Journey to Jo'burg, Beverley Naidoo (Longman Knockouts). (9-12 year-olds).Naledi and Tiro's mother works away from home. She is employed as a servant by a white family in Johannesburg. Their younger sister becomes very ill and the two children journey to the big city to fetch their mother. The visit to Johannesburg, the stay in Soweto and encounters with her mother's employer and the police open Naledi's eyes to the whole South African experience. The story offers a simple, direct introduction to the issues of apartheid.

Comfort Herself, Geraldine Kaye (Deutsch). (10-12 year olds). The heroine of this story, Comfort Kwatey-Jones, has a white English mother and a Ghanaian father. After the death of her mother in a road accident, Comfort experiences a series of moves to a children's home, to a village in Kent with her white grandparents, and to both rural and urban Ghana.

Leslyn in London, Grace Nichols (Hodder and Stoughton). (8-10 year olds). Leslyn moves from the warmth and security of Guyana to live with her father in London. Initially her experiences are not pleasant; she hates the cold, the big city and the racism at school. Gradually, however, she begins to adjust and settle down.

Resources

Black Settlers in Britain 1555-1958, File and Power (Heinemann).
World Studies 8-13, Fisher and Hicks (Oliver and Boyd). This contains details of the Word House game.
Refugees (Save the Children Fund). This is an excellent pack with background information and pupil activities.
Rafa Rafa, Garry Shirts (Christian Aid).
They Came to Britain, Page (Edward Arnold). This is a useful account of the various groups which make up the British people.

Italians to Britain: 1950s. Many Italian workers were recruited to come to this country after the Second World War. There was a shortage of labour in industry. Many decided to stay and settle.

Normans to England: 1066. William the Conqueror defeated Harold and the Saxons at the battle of Hastings. As a result the Normans seized English lands.

Vietnamese to Britain: 1970s and 1980s. Many Vietnamese families decided they wanted to leave Vietnam to seek a better life in the West. They escaped from Vietnam often in small boats.

Commonwealth citizens to the UK: 1950s and 1960s. Many people came from the West Indies, India, Pakistan and other countries. Britain needed workers for industry, transport etc.

Figure 2

Languages and communication

British attitudes to other languages tend to be negative. Languages seem to be arranged in a scale of grudging acceptability. There is often apathy towards the learning of European languages, perhaps as a result of insularity and a sense of misplaced superiority. Attitudes towards other more 'exotic' languages often include definite antipathy, hostility and racism. It must surely be the case, however, that if we do not respect another person's language, which is after all a key part of what makes them a special, unique individual, then it is very possible that our general attitude towards them is negative.

Any theme or topic on language and communication must address these issues. The aim must be to increase respect, awareness and interest in language.

A topic on language could include work on the following themes:
• Writing systems, including hieroglyphs, alphabets, sounds, symbols and calligraphy.
• Cultural variety, including jargon, accent and dialect.
• Language variety, including world languages, languages in Great Britain, languages in the local community and school.
• Common experiences, including greetings, family relations, naming systems, counting and ceremonies.
• Signs and symbols, including cave drawings, picture languages, codes, wordless signs and numbers.

Activity one

Greetings

This is an excellent starter activity and is simple to organise. It is also a useful way of organising children into groups for other activities.

Each child is given a card. On one side is the word for 'hello' written in red in the script of another language. On the other side the word is written in green in an English transcription to show how it is pronounced. Randomly distributed around the room are three sets of larger cards, one set showing the names of the languages represented, another with 'hello' in the scripts of the different languages, and the third with the English transcriptions. The children are told that they've got the word for 'hello' in another language and, if they need it, in the English transcription. The object of the game is to find their partner or partners, but to do so they're only allowed to say the word for 'hello', not showing the card or gesturing. When they are satisfied that they've found the other members of their language group, they go and stand by the green card which has the English transcription of their word. The teacher can go around each group saying hello and inviting the appropriate response.

The next step is for one member of the group to go and fetch the red script sign and put it above the other. Then the group has to guess or decide which language they were speaking and bring over the card with the appropriate language name. The teacher can supply clues if necessary.

Activity two

We want to be your friends and live in peace

This is an activity based on an idea from the Centre for Global Education in York, which is a source of a number of excellent ideas to develop a global perspective.

The idea is very simple. Groups of children are given a sealed envelope with a message in it. The message reads 'We want to be your friends and live in peace'. Give each group the same message, but let them think they have different messages. The groups are then asked to imagine that they are going to meet the other groups, and they have to communicate their messages using only the medium they are given. This could be paper and crayons, musical instruments, their own bodies, sticky paper, clay, Plasticine or puppets. Stress that they cannot use numbers or letters and that the other groups do not understand English.

Give each group a separate area to work in and an allocated time, perhaps 20 minutes. When the groups are ready, ask them to take turns to present their message while the others try to understand. In most cases the other groups will make reasonable guesses, and they will usually make sense of what is presented.

Follow-up discussions can include ideas about the need for a common language, the ease with which misunderstandings can arise, and the importance of trying to see what people have to say before we make judgements.

Activity three
Language survey
It is often assumed that only schools with Asian children will show evidence of bilingualism among the children and their families. I have conducted language surveys in a number of all-white schools which entirely disprove this. Children themselves often discover a linguistic heritage of which they were unaware.

It is important that the survey always asks questions about grandparents. The answers to these questions often give evidence of migration patterns within the areas during the 1930s and 1940s.

Once completed the survey should provide a wealth of fascinating statistics. These can be interpreted and displayed as bar charts, pie charts, on a database or as percentages. There should be ample enthusiasm for further research into the languages, such as ways to say hello and welcome or perhaps a tape recording of the family speaking together.

Above all, any survey like this can raise important questions among children and staff about our attitudes to languages. Why is it that by the time of the third generation many languages are no longer being used? I am thinking particularly of Irish, Welsh, Ukranian and other European languages. How much value do teachers place on bilingualism?

Activity four
Languages of Britain
This is a natural follow-up to a class or school survey. Children should know something of the linguistic make-up of Britain. Britain is not monolingual. ILEA has recorded over 100 languages spoken in London schools. Over 64 languages are spoken in Coventry schools.

For this activity you will need a set of 30 to 40 cards. Divide these into sub-sets of three or four, each sub-set representing a different British city, for example Glasgow, Coventry, Leeds and Cardiff. The cards can contain basic or more complicated information as in Figure 3. Each city should show evidence of different languages. Share the cards

Coventry
Punjabi
Many people from Punjab came to Coventry in the 1950s and 1960s to work. Punjabi is spoken mainly in Punjab, India.

Figure 3

out randomly among the children, then ask them to find out who lives in the same city as them. Ask them to form groups based on this information. This done, each group can do a number of tasks such as recording their language on a class wall map or display, tabulating the reasons people moved to their city, researching more about the language or finding out one or two words of the relevant language.

Activity five

Language hunt

This is fairly simple to organise once you have the basic information. The idea is that a number of key areas or rooms in the school acquire signs in English and another language. The acquisition of those other languages can itself be an excellent way of using the linguistic varieties within the schools. Once made, the signs could remain permanently.

The language hunt could take various forms. A typical task sheet is shown in Figure 4. For younger children written clues could be given as to the names of the languages.

Activity six

Language taster

This activity requires careful preparation beforehand but is well worth the effort. Four or five children are withdrawn from the class for about three 15-minute sessions and turned into teachers of another language. The children then work with a small group of their peers and 'teach' them. The session can be organised so that each child gets a taste of two languages.

The actual amount of language should be limited. Perhaps simply 'Hello, I'm...' and 'Goodbye'. What is important is that there should be a fair representation of different languages. For many children there is a scale of respect for other languages. In the all-white school the child teaching Punjabi or Bengali to his peers might do something, albeit very small, to improve the status of that language.

Once the children have experienced a taste of the languages this could be recorded, or it might even form the basis for an assembly on language.

Resources

Awareness of Language, editor Eric Hawkins (Cambridge Educational). The series comprises the following titles: *Get the Message, How Language Works, Spoken and Written Language, Using Language, Language Varieties and Change, How do we Learn Languages* and *Awareness of Language*. It is a practical background book for teachers. A cassette is also available.
The Language Book, Mike Raleigh (ILEA

Language Hunt

There are ten new signs displayed around the school. When you find them copy down the information. Try and find out the other languages.

Sign in English	Sign in Other Language	Name of Language
1. Office	Bureau	French
2.		
3.		

Figure 4

English Centre). This contains a wealth of useful ideas.

Introduction to Language, Aplin et al (Hodder and Stoughton). This contains a sections on the history of European languages, writing, language families and animal language.

Language and Languages, Derek Strange (Oxford University Press). This aims to develop pupils' awareness of language, increase their understanding of English and stimulate their interest in other languages.

The Children's Language Project, London Institute of Education (Philograph Publications). This is a useful pack with resources and ideas on various topics: *Language at home, Languages at school, Languages around us, Languages near and far* and an *Introduction to languages*.

Images and information

The National Curriculum Consultation document 5-11 (*The Cox Report*) declared that media studies were central in developing major aspects of English through:

• The understanding of how meanings are constructed in different media: literature, film and television, newspapers etc and how different interpretations of the same text are possible.

• Concepts such as audience, convention, author, editor, selection (of information, viewpoint etc), stereotype, etc.

• The understanding of stereotypes: questions of accuracy, realism, fiction, different points of view, persuasive and partial uses of language.

There are clear implications here for multicultural perspectives. Any topic on the media should include reference to:

• Lack of representation in the media of minority groups.

• Images of developing countries in books and on television.

• How to recognise stereotypes and resist perpetuating them.

• How to increase children's power of criticism.

• The offering of poor and inaccurate information in school.

• The language of the media.

There follows a number of activities which could be used as starting points for raising some of these issues.

Activity one

The Peters Projection

Try and create a mental map of the world in your head, and now answer this question. Which is bigger, Greenland or Australia? For most teachers I believe the answer will be Greenland. The mental map we carry in our heads is based on the Mercator Projection. Like most teachers I was brought up with this. The correct answer to the question is, of course, that Australia is about three times bigger than Greenland. The reason for this mistake is that Mercator's projection is accurate in shape but not in size. There are many other inaccuracies. Africa appears to be a Southern continent, whereas in fact most of Africa is in the northern hemisphere. Britain seems to be almost on the Equator. The reaction by some teachers to this may be 'so what?'. I believe, however, that this is a classic example of how we are willing to accept false information and to continue to make use of it. We offer this false information to children every time we use an atlas or do any work with a world map. So what are the alternatives? The world is a sphere, so it is naturally impossible to reproduce it in total accuracy on flat paper. But there are alternative projections.

The Peters Projection was first produced in 1962 by Arno Peters for UNICEF. This projection distorts shape but is accurate in terms of size. It can be used as the basis for the following activity.

Begin the session by showing the net of a cube and how it can be assembled to produce a solid shape. Next set the children a simple task. With a sheet paper they are to make a net of their own head which can be assembled by the teacher. The teacher can reassure them over minor details like ears; the main task should be to reproduce the general shape. The children's initial reaction may well be that it is impossible but it will not be long before they apply themselves with great inventiveness and ingenuity. Some wrap the sheet around their heads, others request adhesive tape (sorry, it must flatten out into a net!), others will work on the segment theory and come close to success. After a suitable time spent on this the teacher can pull the session together and look at the various efforts. When the teacher asks the question 'Why was it impossible?' most children will realise that it was because their heads are basically round.

The teacher can then bring the discussion round to maps. What is the problem for the map-maker? Paper is flat and the world is round. Three or four questions can then be put on the board, on the lines of 'Which is bigger, Australia or Greenland?', 'Is Britain towards the top or the middle of the earth?'. Pass a globe around the class and ask the children to find out. Bring out the Mercator Projection map and ask the children to answer the same questions and compare the answers.

The Peters Projection map can then be offered and discussed as an alternative. This activity can raise all sorts of questions about believing everything you are told or read or see.

Follow-up work could include looking at maps from other countries. Maps of America show America in the centre of the world. Maps of New Zealand likewise. For many children this is fascinating and totally unexpected.

Activity two

Stereotypes

The danger of activities that seek to raise awareness and destroy stereotypes is that they often have the effect of reinforcing those images. Inviting children to draw or describe the typical Irishman, Chinese or Indian is often done with the best of intentions but unless the discussion and follow-up activities are carefully handled the children can be left only with the memory of the lovingly constructed stereotype, which remains as the one true image. The following activity could also have this effect, but is worth trying when dealt with carefully.

For this activity you will need to make two sets of cards: one with nationalities or ethnic groups and the other with characteristics or traits that are considered to be stereotypical. Share the cards among the class and ask the children to find the person whose card belongs with theirs. Ask them to record their findings. Collect the cards, shuffle them and repeat the exercise. This can be done a third time. The information can then be transferred to the blackboard in matrix form. What should emerge is some pattern of stereotypes. Ethiopians will

almost always be matched with 'can't help themselves'; the English emerge as 'sportsmanlike'. There will not always be a consistent match but there will be enough material to work on.

The next step is to ask the children if they have ever had contact through their family or friends with any of the nationalities represented. Provided the examples are not too obscure there will usually be some contact with most. Those children can then be asked what the real people were like and whether the stereotypical characteristic was true of them. Step by step all the stereotypes will be knocked down.

The final step can again be centred round two sets of cards. One set will have a number of characteristics, while on the other will be the word 'British', hidden by a peel-off sticker. Both sets will be lettered. The children then find the person whose card matches theirs: A-A, B-B and so on. When the pairs have been formed there can be speculation as to which nationality is beneath the sticker. Finally the sticker

can be pulled off to reveal the word 'British'.

The children can then discuss the implications and will undoubtedly come up with conclusions such as 'There's good and bad in everyone'.

Activity three

Media analysis

Analysing photographs within newspapers can provide children with hard statistical evidence of how views, images and stereotypes can be formed subconsciously in all of us. Given that over half the population are women, that there are over two million black people in Britain and that there are significant numbers of disabled people, how fairly and accurately are these represented in the visual images offered to us by newspapers purporting to report across the whole of society?

As an initial activity the children worked in pairs, each with a newspaper. Their task was to analyse every photograph in that newspaper, recording their information as follows:

Photograph 1:
No. of men
No. of women
No. of Asian men
No. of Afro-Caribbean men
No. of Asian women
No. of Afro-Caribbean women
No. of disabled.

The task could be made shorter by giving each pair a number of pages rather than a whole newspaper. The analysis of the photographs could also be broadened to include the roles being played by the figures in the photographs. Do the majority of photographs of women appear in advertisements? Are black people usually only to be found on sports pages?

The activity could be further extended by conducting an analysis of two different papers, one 'quality' newspaper and one tabloid, over a period of one or two weeks. Pairs of children could be given responsibility for each day's collection of results.

Resources

Images of Africa, Action Aid.
Making Stories, ILEA.
Changing Stories, ILEA.

Food

A topic based on food seems a natural place for multicultural initiatives. It is too easy, however, to suppose that introducing the class to different tastes and experiences will have the desired effect. Many children have an in-built resistance to the new or unusual.

Persuading children not to react with a 'Yuk!' or 'No way am I trying that!' can often be the main thrust of the theme. It is to be hoped that even breaking down this barrier might be a small contribution to increasing awareness and tolerance of others. Introducing unfamiliar fruit and vegetables is probably a pointless exercise unless the intention is to lead children towards a more reasoned acceptance of things which are beyond their immediate experience.

I believe that a topic on food should include reference to:
• Environmental issues such as additivies, pesticides etc.
• Issues of justice and fairness and food as a basic human right and need.
• Issues of hunger and aid. Why are there food mountains?
• Positive references to the contribution different ethnic groups have made to eating habits in Britain.
• Healthy eating and the pressures put on children by the major food companies.

There follows some activities to help raise these issues.

Activity one

Globingo

At first glance this might seem to have little to do with food, but in fact the game is intended to demonstrate to children that we all have countless links with the rest of the world, many more than we imagine. These links can be through the people we know, the music we listen to, the clothes we wear and the food we eat.

The game is based on an idea by Johnson and Benegar. I have used the version available in *Global Teacher, Global Learner* by Pike and Selby.

One way of beginning the activity is to let the children see actual links between

Who has relatives in another country?	Who can speak a language other than English?	Who has visited another country?
Julia Narinder Rebecca Rashed Katy	Siân Rashed Julia	Michael Julia Rashed Natasha Daniel
Who is wearing something made in another country?	**Who has a penfriend in another country?**	**Who has eaten food from another country today?**
Katy Paul Narinder James Siân	Natasha Katy	Daniel Rashed Michael Katy Rebecca James

Figure 5

different areas of the world. For this I use a large ball of wool. To start with, a question is asked such as 'Who's got a relative living in another country?'. One child who has a relative living elsewhere in the world is chosen, and the wool is tied round her wrist. Another question is then asked, such as 'Who's wearing something made in another country?'. Another child becomes attached by the wool. This continues, and if necessary some questions are repeated until the whole class is linked. It might seem a recipe for chaos but it is an extremely effective way of showing our global connections.

Once this is finished the children are given the questions in written form and have to go round the class asking each class member a different question. It is an excellent co-operative activity. The winner is the first to complete the questions. They can unravel the wool!

A full list of all the countries mentioned can then be drawn up. The children will be astonished by the total. This information could then be displayed in the classroom. Each child could have a number of small cards to complete, for example, 'Narinder is wearing shoes made in Italy'. These could be arranged around a world map. The information could also be presented in the form of a grid, as in Figure 5.

Activity two
The world in a supermarket bag
This activity would naturally follow a session of Globingo. The intention is to

reinforce children's understanding of how the foods we buy have an effect on the lives of people living elsewhere in the world. The activity also raises issues such as advertising and the creation of demand, and packaging. It was devised by Oxfam's Education Department, who produce an excellent range of materials.

Provide the children with supermarket bags full of food tins and packets. Ask them to work in groups and unpack the bag, identifying the origin and cost of each item. Ask the groups to display the food attractively with labels, and present their information to the rest of the class.

The children can then produce small information cards about the food which can be matched to countries on a large world map for classroom display. Ask the children to analyse their food in more depth. Which food cost most? Which food cost least? Why is some food more expensive than others? The Oxfam pack suggests a wide range of follow-up activities. The contents of the bag could be varied to meet the needs of any topic. I have used the activity successfully to

show how we depend on rainforest products for so much of the quality of our everyday life.

Activity three

The World Feast game

The World Feast game is produced by Christian Aid. It takes a great deal of preparation and is best done during a whole morning or afternoon session. It is, however, well worth it. In a very dramatic manner it offers children an insight into the inequality of food distribution throughout the world.

Tell the children that they are going first to produce food, and then to share in a world feast. Divide the class into groups representing a food-producing area of the world: Europe, North America, Russia, Africa, Asia, Latin America and China. Ask the groups to produce a specific number of food items on paper to put into the global pot. Different groups have different resources including scissors, pencils, adhesive etc, as well as money. The resources must be bought and traded between areas if they are to have the means to produce the feast. Each area has its own production target to meet. For example, Africa must produce 20 items of fruit, while North America's target is two cereal items. All the food items are displayed on a large mural.

Once this is completed the money is counted and then it is time for the real feast. This consists of bread, corned beef, fruit, cereal, milk, tea and rice. At this stage there is clearly a great deal of excitement and anticipation. The teacher then distributes the food in the proportions directed by the game rules. There is an obvious unbalance between the rewards of the different areas: Africa worked for the whole session and produced plenty of fruit, and yet it receives only one bowl of cereal, whereas North America worked for a very short period but receives almost half of the total global feast. The children's reactions will include anger, disappointment and almost certainly moral outrage. 'Why did they start with most money, finish with even more money, and get all the food, when they only had to do a little bit of what we had to do?'

The activity will hopefully be the starting point for further discussion of some of the issues. It is usually the case that the two areas with most food, Europe and North America, do offer to share their feast with the others. This raises interesting questions around the subject of aid. How generous are those two areas being in giving back something that wasn't theirs by right in the first place?

Other activities around the theme of food could include:
• Photograph work. There are excellent collections of photographs available from E J Arnold and Galt. These could be used with any of the activities suggested in

Chapter Three. Looking at different 'food' stories and folk tales from round the world. The same story has often appears in different countries in only a slightly different form, such as the Magic Pasta Pot and the Magic Porridge Pot.
• Looking at the significance of food in different faiths.
• Conducting a survey of different take-away food shops, looking at the different foods on offer.
• Finding out the names for such basic foods as bread and milk in different languages.
• Having visitors to do simple cookery demonstrations, but beware of stereotyping the Asian mum as 'the Chapati lady'.
• Investigating different sorts of bread such as pitta, croissants and baguettes. Why are they all available in Britain? How do they differ? Collecting food labels from different products and investigating the language and country of origin.

Resources

World in a Supermarket Bag, Oxfam.
World Feast Game, Christian Aid.
Global Teacher, Global Learner, Pike and Selby (Hodder and Stoughton). Contains details of Globingo.
What Do We Eat? (Centre for World Development Education). This is a computer database to help children analyse their food intake and compare it with that of a country they have chosen to base their project on. The package contains an A5 booklet and a 40-track disc.
Disasters in the Classroom (Oxfam) is an excellent pack which looks at underlying causes of 'disasters' and encourages children to challenge stereotypes.
Exploring Foods (Mantra Books) There are two books in the series: *Exploring Indian Food in Britain*, and *Exploring Chinese Food in Britain*. They are packed with colour illustrations, photographs and recipes.

Focus On Series (Wayland). The series includes books on coffee, rice, fruit, meat, grain, seafood, sugar and tea.
Food and Drink Series (Wayland). Each book covers the food and drinks of one country and explains how food is grown and processed and how it is prepared, cooked and served. Places covered include Britain, the Caribbean, China, France, Greece, India, Italy, Japan, Mexico, the Middle East, North America, Russia, South East Asia and Spain.
Food Series (Wayland). This is an attractive series with a strong multicultural focus. Topics include bread, eggs, milk, potatoes, beans and pulses, fish, fruit, meat, rice, sugar and vegetables.
Mixed Vegetables: a First Look at Vegetables, and *Fruit Salad: a First Look at Fruit*, Julia Eccleshare (Hamish Hamilton). Two excellent little books which include both familiar and less well-known produce.

Chapter Seven

Ideas for topics

The previous chapter described in detail various teaching activities that could be used to initiate, support or develop the themes outlined. Many of those activities could easily be adapted to suit other themes, particularly the ones which aim to raise general awareness.

In this chapter, I propose to look at several more popular classroom themes and suggest some ways to incorporate multicultural perspectives and dimensions. It is impossible for every session or every day in the classroom to achieve everything which could or should be achieved. It is more realistic to accept that there will be certain elements which are readily identifiable as multicultural. At other times the multicultural dimension

might simply be within the resource materials used in the classroom, such as positive photographs of a multi-racial Britain.

Water

Religion and myths
A topic based on water could include the use of water in religious ceremonies. Water has a special significance for many of the faith groups in Britain. These include baptism for Christians, wuzu (ritual washing before prayers), the Sikh naming

ceremony, and the significance of the River Ganges for Hindus. Look at the significance and symbolism of water in the myths of various cultures, for example Noah's Ark or the Descent of the Ganges.

The need for water

A broader study could include a discussion of water as a basic human need. The children could 'brainstorm' various uses of water and prioritise them. Encourage discussion of water as a basic human right. Point out that 51 per cent of the world's population does not have access to safe water. Why is this so? Whose fault is it? It can be difficult to avoid giving children the impression that it is somehow the fault of these people that they have no safe water. It is clearly impossible to explain complex economic questions of debt and repayment to young children but there could be clear indication that many nations have the means to share the world's resources.

Water and the media

Look at the way countries which experience drought are portrayed in the media. We are bombarded with pictures of drought in Africa, but children should be offered another side of the picture. Looking at drought and its effects should be offset by pointing out that not all of Africa is desert. Use photograph activities to present another view.

Language

Water supplies in developing countries are often described as 'dirty' or 'unclean' as compared to the 'clean' water of developed nations. The negative connotations of 'dirty' and 'unclean' can be subconsciously transferred to the people who live in those countries. Use words like 'safe' and 'unsafe', which is in fact a more accurate description.

Taking water for granted

It is difficult for most children in Britain to imagine life without easy access to a tap. However, it is a fact that many women in other parts of the world spend a large part of their day carrying water home over long distances. Show the children a picture of a woman in an African setting carrying a bucket or water jar on her head. The reaction may well be one of amusement. Give the children the opportunity to share this experience by

carrying a heavy bucket of water in their hands. This can be timed. Repeat the experiment with the bucket held on the head. This is best done outside with the children wearing waterproof clothing. It might seem a superficial way of trying to reconstruct a laborious task but it could open children's eyes a little.

The question of carrying water will also raise important questions of gender. Why is it the women who always carry the water? What would they do all day if they didn't have this chore?

Water and hygiene

Give the children a simple chart on which to record the number of times they use the toilet, take a bath or shower, wash up, fill a bottle etc. Ask them to translate this into gallons of water. One class of primary children were astonished to find they used over a million gallons per year!

Resources

Focus on Water Project Pack (Christian Aid). This contains background information, visual material, photographs and case studies of development projects.
Going Upstream (UNICEF). This is a water game which aims to heighten awareness of hygiene and water usage.
The Water Game, Centre for World Development Education (CWDE). This is a computer program based on the daily use and supply of water.
Water is Life...and Safe Water Means Better Life (CWDE). This is an excellent World Health Organisation wallchart.
Children Need Water, Wendy Davies (Wayland). A useful information book produced in association with Save the Children.

Rainforests

Ecological issues are very much in the news at present and many excellent educational materials are available from various pressure groups and organisations.

Exploring children's images

The power of the media is such that for many children the term 'rainforest' as opposed to 'jungle' is readily accepted and used. It is still worthwhile, however, to spend some time on the impressions children have about rainforests and jungles. Ask children to write down the word jungle in the middle of a piece of paper and surround it with their visual and written images. It's guaranteed that the pages will be full of tigers, snakes, Tarzans, cannibals, natives and words such as 'primitive', 'fierce' and 'savage'. This can be extended usefully by talking about where their images come from and how realistic they are.

Positive views

Present the rainforest people in a positive way and encourage the children to look beyond the immediate superficial differences. This will not be easy, but the activity 'Rafa Rafa', as described in Chapter Six, could be used to show how cultural bridges can be crossed, provided there is a willingness to communicate.

The importance of the rainforest

Encourage the children to look at our dependence on rainforest products. This could be done using a similar activity to 'The world in a supermarket bag' as outlined in Chapter Six. Teachers should have no difficulty in assembling a number of shopping bags with various rainforests products.

Resources

Yanomamo, a musical by Peter Rose and Ann Conlon and published by the Worldwide Fund for Nature, looks at the central issues surrounding rainforests and their destruction.

Rainforest Child, a learning pack for eight to 13-year-olds, is available from Greenlight Publications. It comprises a teacher's handbook and numerous activities. Contact Greenlight Publications, Ty Bryn, Coomb Gardens, Llangynog, Carmarthen, Dyfed SA33 5AY.

Rainforests Resource Pack is available from the Centre for World Development Education. It is produced by Living Earth and includes posters and notes.

The Romans

'The Romans' or 'Roman Britain' might not initially seem an ideal starting point for developing multicultural perspectives relevant to British schoolchildren in twentieth century Britain. However, if we accept that within all areas of learning there are opportunities to raise multicultural issues, it should be possible to identify certain strands which should appear in any consideration of the Romans and their influence. It is possible to do this naturally, without risking accusations of contrivance.

Language

The Romans brought Latin with them to Britain and this was the accepted language of the Empire. It was not, however, the only language: the vast majority of citizens of the Roman Empire were bilingual. Twentieth century Britain also has many citizens who are bilingual and this should be seen as a positive thing. There should be many opportunities here to look at community languages in Britain, and our attitudes to other languages. Why do we feel threatened by another language? Is it right to expect people to give up their language?

The English language is made up of

borrowings from many other languages including Celtic, Latin, French and so on. Children could investigate the various language groups which have contributed to English. The Word House game described in Chapter Six could be used.

We base our script on the Roman alphabet. Children could look at different scripts and alphabets, particularly those used in Britain. There are many dual language books available now to use as examples.

The legacy of the Romans

Like all people who move, whether for conquest, in search of new opportunities or from fear, the Romans left their mark on the everyday life and culture of Britain. The Roman army and later settlers brought new food, clothing, language, crafts, businesses and so on. It is natural to draw a parallel between this and the many obvious examples of contributions made by groups who have settled in Britain during the twentieth century.

Celtic resistance and acceptance

The Romans were not welcomed with open arms. They were met with violent resistance and hostility. This was not surprising, as they were invaders. What was the effect of this culture clash? Did a gradual acceptance of difference and similarity emerge, leading to a more peaceful co-existence?

With an older class it should not be difficult to raise questions of our acceptance of strangers and newcomers to the school, and to discuss in broader terms the arrival of different minority groups to a country. Ask the children to compare and discuss the different reasons people might have for moving to another country; to invade, to trade, as refugees, as settlers, and so on.

The composition of the Empire

The Romans were not a homogenous group of people, and they did not all share the same language, customs or lifestyle. The differences were far more obvious than the similarities. We tend to visualise the stereotypical toga-clad senator or the white legionary, but the Roman Empire included people from Africa, Turkey, Spain and Israel. There is strong evidence that many black soldiers from what is now Morocco served in Britain.

It is important to point out to children that it was possible for all these different people to live together under the Roman Empire. Furthermore the Roman Empire did not demand that they abandon their own language, culture and all the other things which made them unique.

Homes

Houses, homes and buildings are frequent classroom themes, and are often viewed as obvious and fertile areas in which multicultural ideas can develop. Looking at the varieties of building styles and materials would offer countless opportunities to celebrate the richness of human achievement.

There can, however, often be a temptation to offer children the 'houses and homes around the world' experience with all its attendant drawbacks. Ask any children to list three words associated with Inuit people and they will undoubtedly include igloo. Similarly for most children travellers live in caravans and Africans, by and large, live in mud huts. The images offered by television, books and comics have done little to dispel the erroneous stereotypes and generalisations which are simply not relevant to the modern world. While it may be true to say that some Inuit have retained the traditional skills of building snow houses, it is far more accurate and truthful to portray them as occupying western-style houses. A topic around this area could include several aspects supporting the broader definition of a multicultural curriculum.

Similarities of experience

Houses may look different and may appear to be better or worse, but it is important for children to look beyond these obvious differences and to realise that every house is a home for someone whether it is a run down housing estate or a penthouse suite. Encouraging children to think beyond the instant value judgement is essential.

Justice and fairness

When children see images of shanty towns in the Third World, tent cities in Ethiopia or decaying tower blocks in inner city areas the initial reaction can often be one of distaste and superiority. Teachers have a responsibility to challenge these images and to begin to develop a critical awareness of the reasons why these situations have arisen.

The global context

How many times is Calcutta used to depict scenes of poor quality housing and homelessness? How often is this picture balanced with photographs of other parts of India? If it isn't, then the children may retain a one-sided image of India. How much does this contribute to the western notion of superiority, and a corresponding negative attitude towards the children in our schools with an Asian background? Suggesting that houses in Britain are all perfect is equally inaccurate.

The experience of travellers

The Swann Report argued that in view of the extreme prejudice and hostility they faced, Gypsies in particular can be seen as 'a group of immigrants still not fully accepted by their host countries after four or five hundred years of occupation'.

Resources

Moving On is a pack which looks at the problems faced by travelling people. It is available from the Minority Rights Group. *Doorways* is a pack which raises issues of homelessness. It is available from Save the Children.

Useful addresses

Local authority centres

These can offer information and advice on resources. Many operate a lending service and some produce their own materials.

Avon
Multicultural Education Centre, Bishop Road, Bristol B57 8LS.
Barking and Dagenham
Language Unit, London Borough of Barking and Dagenham, Station Parade, East Street, Barking, Essex.
Bedfordshire
Resources Centre, Acacia Road, Bedford MK42 OHU.
Berkshire
Support Service for Language and Intercultural Education, Lydford Road, Reading RG1 5QH.
Birmingham
Multicultural Support Service, Bordesey Centre, Camp Hill, Stratford Road, Birmingham B11 1AR.
Bradford
Multicultural Education Service, T F Davies Teachers' Centre, Roasemount, Clifton Villas, Bradford BD8 7BY.
Coventry
Minority Group Support Service, Southfields Old School, Southfields, Coventry CV1 5EJ.
Haringey
Multicultural Curriculum Development Unit, St Mary's C of E Junior School, Rectory Gardens, London N8 7PJ.
Harrow
Multicultural Support Service, Little Stanmore First and Middle School, St David's Drive, Edgware, Middlesex HA8 6JA.
Hounslow
CSL Unit, Smallberry Green Centre, London Road, Isleworth, Middlesex TW3 4DW.
Humberside
Multicultural Resource Unit, Scunthorpe Teachers' Centre, 34 High Street, Scunthorpe, Lincs.
Kent
Multicultural Education Resources Centre, Chantry School, Ordnance Road, Gravesend, Kent DA12 2RL.
Lancashire
Minority Ethnic Group Support Service, 103 Preston New Road, Blackburn, Lancashire.
Leeds
Concord Multifaith Resources, Elmhurst Centre, Newton Road, Leeds LS7 2HE.
Leicestershire
Multicultural Service, Rushey Mead Centre, Harrison Road, Leicester LE4 7PA.
Liverpool
Multiracial Education Service, Crown Street, Liverpool L7 3EA.
Lothian
Multicultural Education Centre, Lothian Outdoor Education Centre, McDonald Road, Edinburgh EH7 4LD.
Manchester
Multicultural Development Service, Greenhams Centre, Upper Lloyd Street, Manchester M14 4HY.
Newnham
Multicultural Support Team In-Service Education Centre, New City School,

Plaistow, London E13 9PY.

Northamptonshire
Multicultural Education Service, C/O Cliftonville Middle School, Cliftonville Road, Northampton NN1 5BW.

Oldham
Multicultural Education and Language Service, Greengate Centre, Greengate Street, Oldham OL4 1RY.

Oxfordshire
Centre for Multicultural Education, East Oxford First School, Union Street, Oxford OX4 1JP.

Rochdale
English Language Support Service, Fieldhouse School, Greenbank Road, Rochdale, Lancashire.

Sandwell
Ethnic Minorities Support Service, Teachers' Centre, Churchbridge, Oldbury, Warley, West Midlands B69 2AX.

Walsall
Intercultural Curriculum Support Service, Gorway Block, Walsall WS1 3BD.

Wolverhampton
Multicultural Education Service Resources Centre, Bellminster House, Birches Barn Road, Penn Fields, Wolverhampton WV3 7BJ.

Charities

Most of these charities have excellent education departments which produce catalogues of resources. The materials are always reasonably priced.

Action Aid, Hamlyn House, Archway, London N19 5PS.

Catholic Fund for Overseas Development (CAFOD), 2 Romero Close, Stockwell Road, London SW9 9TY.

Christian Aid, PO Box 100, London SE1 7RT.

Oxfam, 274 Banbury Road, Oxford OX2 7DZ.

Save the Children Fund, Mary Batchelor House, 17 Grove Lane, London SE5 8RD.

Traidcraft, Kingsway, Teme Valley Trading Estate, Gateshead NE11 ONE.

UNICEF, 55-56 Lincoln's Inn Fields, London WC2A 3NB.

War on Want, 37-39 Great Guildford Street, London SE1 OES.

World Wide Fund for Nature (WWF), Panda House, Weyside Park, Godalming, Surrey GU7 1XR.

Bookshops and suppliers

Baker Book Services Ltd, Manfield Park, Guildford Road, Cranleigh, Surrey GU6 8NU.

Bladestock Publications, Unit 1, 124-128 Brixton Hill, London SW2 1RS.

Gemini Teaching Aids, 19 Kirkgate, Sherburn-in-Elmet, Leeds LS25 6BH.

Hummingbird Book Services, 136 Grosvenor Road, Bristol BS2 8YA.

Invicta Book Services, 162 Coppice Street, Oldham, Lancashire OL8 4BJ.

Jennie Ingham Associates, Purnell Distribution Centre, Poulton, Bristol BS18 5LQ.

Raddles Bookshop, 70 Berners Street, Leicester LE2 OAF.

Soma Books, Commonwealth Institute, Kensington High Street, London W8 6NQ.

Third World Publications, 151 Stratford Road, Birmingham B11 1RD.

Walter Rodney Bookshop, 5A Chignell Place, Ealing, London W13 OTJ.